THE **ELEPHANT** in the **ROOM**

Everyone's pain when the U.S. Dollar devalues again…

B.Y. LEO

THE ELEPHANT in the ROOM
Everyone's pain when the U.S. Dollar devalues again…

CONTENTS

A Note from the Author

Chapter 1   Raison d'être

Chapter 2   Exit the British Pound and Enter the U.S. Dollar

Chapter 3   Collusion, Collaboration, Clashes and Disputes

Chapter 4   Economic Evolution and Crisis Management

Chapter 5   Tremors, More Tremors and Continued Audacity

Chapter 6   Bracing and Preparing for the Demise

References

Suggested Reading List

Study Notes

About the Author

A Note from the Author

The world grows ever more complex with rising geopolitical tensions in an increasingly interconnected global economy. Amid these shifts, a seismic transformation is quietly unfolding in international finance. Its significance is often overlooked, and yet, when it comes to fruition, the impact will be profound (and far-reaching?). No one will remain untouched and while there may be no place to hide, there are ways to prepare to mitigate the pain.

This *"Elephant in the Room"* is about the gradual but undeniable decline of the U.S. Dollar as the world's reserve currency, a subject that, while whispered about, seldom draws the concern it warrants. My aim in writing this book is to bridge the gap between the intricate workings of international finance and the lives of everyday people. What happens in the global financial arena has direct consequences for each of us, affecting our daily lives in ways we may not yet realise.

In these pages, I aim to simplify the complexities of finance, distilling jargon into relatable terms, drawing analogies to historical events and presenting evidence to support my findings. I've woven in lessons from financial history, insights from my research, and, in places, a light-hearted touch to keep the narrative engaging.

This endeavour would not have been possible without the support and guidance of many. My heartfelt gratitude goes first to Koh Chin Seng, a mentor and friend, whose sharp critique of an article pouring scorn on BRICS scholars and his own clinical insights, sparked the inspiration for this book.

Special thanks to my editor and friend, Danesh Daryanani, whose meticulous efforts shaped this manuscript. To my British friends, Chase French, post-investment banking in Hong Kong, and Stephen McParlin, post-aeronautics at Imperial College London, thank you for your thoughtful reviews and valuable insights that made this work more accessible to the general reader. These collaborations have been yet another milestone in the journey of our friendship.

I am equally indebted to Chua Aik Hong for painstakingly navigating through the drafts, steering the narrative towards clarity and relevance. To Bryan Lam and Sanjiv Koghar, whose introduction to publishers, helping me to understand publishing made this book possible, my deepest thanks.

As you embark on this reading journey, I hope you find it enlightening and thought-provoking. Most importantly, may it inspire you to prepare for the changes ahead and act with informed conviction.

Enjoy the read, embrace the learning and take action.

Warm regards,
B.Y. Leo

Chapter 1
Raison d'etre
The Mighty Role of U.S. Dollar, its Settlement Mechanism and its Dominance...

"*Raison d'être*" in French literally translates to *"reason for being"* in English; the essence or purpose that drives one's existence. For example, Mozart's *raison d'être* was music and opera, Marie Curie's *raison d'être* was *pioneering radiation science and Lionel Messi's raison d'être is football*. A person's raison d'être fuels their motivation and gives meaning to their pursuits.

Could the *raison d'être* of the **United States Dollar (USD)** be to serve as the world's reserve currency? In *"finance speak"*, this means being the dominant and most widely used currency globally, facilitating international trade and ensuring the stability of the global financial system. Since its rise to prominence after World War II, the USD has faithfully fulfilled this demanding role, becoming a cornerstone of the world economy. However, in recent times, cracks have appeared in this dominance, leading to questions about the USD's future role. Discontent and scepticism about its reliability are growing louder.

This book will explore the history of international finance, uncover relevant data, draw analogies and delve into the mechanisms of international trade and exchange rates. Together, we will seek to develop a perspective on whether the USD's *raison d'être* is under threat and what such a shift might mean for the global economy. Preparing for such a transition, whether gradual or abrupt, is imperative, as it could appear unexpectedly, like a thief in the night, catching the world unprepared.

As Karl Marx famously said,
"History repeats itself, first as a tragedy, second as a farce."
While Marx's view may appear grim, I argue that the history of international finance, much like poetry, exhibits rhythmic patterns. These rhythms reflect the peaks and troughs that mark the evolutionary path of global economics, pointing to inevitable shifts in the dynamics of power and currency.

The **United States Dollar (USD)**, commonly referred to as the **"Greenback"**, is universally acknowledged as one of the most influential currencies in the world. Its presence is felt globally, not just as the official currency of the United States but also as a dominant medium of exchange and store of value. While every sovereign nation maintains its own currency for domestic transactions, the USD frequently operates alongside these currencies in numerous countries. In some instances, the USD is so entrenched in local economies that it functions as a de facto currency, widely accepted for trade, savings and investments, underscoring its pivotal role in international finance and commerce.
This raises an intriguing question:
Why does the USD transcend national boundaries?
What makes it so uniquely privileged and widely trusted?

Just a little information snippet about how the "Dollar" got its name: the **"Dollar"** *is said to have been derived from the German monetary unit* **"Taler"**. *It was referenced to the Joachimsthaler, a coin first minted in Jáchymov in 1517.* [1]

Throughout this book, there will be explanations and descriptions referring the United States Dollar as U.S. Dollar, "$" or "USD", the Euro as "EUR", British Pound as "Sterling" or "GBP", Japanese Yen as "JPY" and Chinese renminbi or Yuan as "RMB". We shall reference each currency using its long form name or their three-character moniker.

MIGHTY ROLE OF UNITED STATES DOLLAR

Today, the United States Dollar (USD) is deeply ingrained in global commerce, particularly in the pricing and trading of commodities. On major international commodities exchanges, key resources such as crude oil, precious metals like gold and silver, industrial metals like iron ore and copper and soft commodities such as coffee and sugar are all priced and traded in USD.

The USD's role in international trade extends beyond mere pricing, it underpins critical aspects of global commerce, including:
- ✓ **Price Discovery**: *establishing a universal benchmark for buyers and sellers.*
- ✓ **Trade Flows**: *facilitating seamless global trade transactions.*
- ✓ **Demand and Supply Information**: *acting as a signal for global market trends.*
- ✓ **Liquidity Management**: *offering deep and liquid markets for trading.*
- ✓ **Economic Forecasting**: *providing a stable basis for predicting economic trends.*
- ✓ **Standardisation**: *ensuring uniformity in trade practices across regions.*
- ✓ **Financing**: *serving as a trusted currency for international loans and trade finance.*

These aspects illustrate how the USD embeds itself in the very fabric of international commerce. The USD plays a crucial role in *price discovery*, the process by which traders determine the market price for commodities and decide when to buy or sell. Using the USD as the quoted currency, price discovery establishes a foundation for international trade, helping to reveal patterns of supply and demand within international trade frameworks. This enables participants to gauge whether a commodity is in ample supply, whether it has a buyer's preference, or if it's tilted toward a seller's bias.

With these established frameworks, quasi-governmental and supranational organisations can capture essential trading data that supports *economic forecasting*, helping ensure efficient resource allocation. The *standardisation* of international trading practices, with the USD as the medium of exchange, allows commodities and goods to be priced, invoiced and settled in a regulated manner within established legal frameworks, ensuring consistency and order.

As a result, the USD has become the currency of reference for global trade. Additionally, the USD is vital for the proper functioning of financial markets, enabling investors to easily access deep, liquid USD-denominated fixed-income markets and other assets for investment, portfolio management and reserves management.

To grasp the extent of this dominance, consider the overwhelming trading statistics of three widely traded commodities. These figures highlight the USD's pivotal role in connecting global markets and fostering economic interdependence.

Crude oil is the lifeblood of modern economies, powering industries, transportation and energy systems across the globe. In 2024, global demand for crude oil stood at approximately 100 million barrels per day (bpd). However, this demand is projected to decline to around 93 million bpd by 2030, reflecting shifts toward renewable energy and greater energy efficiency.

A comparison of oil production and consumption highlights significant disparities among major economies. For instance, China, the world's largest crude oil importer, produced only about one-third of its consumption needs in 2022. In contrast, the United States has emerged as the world's largest oil producer, with production nearing 400 million barrels of crude oil per month in recent years. (Figure 1a and 1b). [2]

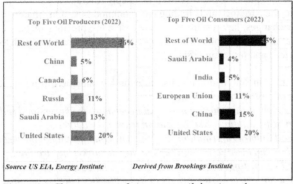

Figure 1a: *China consumes 3 times more oil than it produces.*

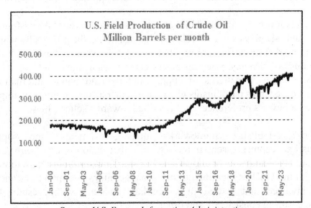

Source: U.S. Energy Information Administration
Figure 1b: *United States became world's largest oil producer in 2022.*

Gold's global demand between 2023 and 2024, averaged approximately 1,200 metric tons per quarter. The two largest sectors driving this demand were jewellery fabrication and jewellery consumption, highlighting gold's enduring cultural and economic significance.

Interestingly, central banks accounted for only about one-fifth of global gold demand during this period. Central banks typically purchase gold to strengthen their physical stockpiles as part of their reserves management portfolios, ensuring financial stability and diversification. [3]

Iron Ore is a critical industrial metal essential for steel production, which drives industries such as construction, engineering, automotive, shipbuilding and machinery. The world's top iron ore producers are Australia and Brazil, with projected production in 2026 expected to reach 940 million tons and 440 million tons, respectively.

The leading global iron ore companies include Vale S.A. from Brazil and Anglo-Australian giants Rio Tinto and BHP. On the consumption side, China has been the dominant driver of global demand, accounting for nearly two-thirds of global iron ore imports from 2010 to 2023. In 2023 alone, China consumed over one billion metric tons of iron ore. However, demand from China is expected to decline to 750 million tons over the next five to ten years due to an economic slowdown, partly linked to an oversupply in the real estate sector.

Iron ore prices, which traded at approximately $100 per dry metric ton in mid-2024, are forecast to fall to $77 by 2026, reflecting reduced demand and changing market dynamics. [4]

Commodity	Monthly Trading	Assumption
Crude Oil	$ 200 billion	based on 100 million bpd for 25 days at USD 80 per barrel
Gold	$ 34 billion	based on 1200 tons per quarter at USD 85 million per ton
Iron Ore	$ 8.3 billion	based on 1 billion tons per year at USD 100 per ton
Total	$ 242.3 billion	

Based on the trading volumes of ***crude oil, gold*** and ***iron ore***, the combined trade volume for these three commodities amounts to approximately ***$242 billion per month***. This staggering figure highlights the scale of USD-denominated transactions occurring globally in international commerce.

The facilitation of such massive trade volumes necessitates a constant flow of USD between counterparties, including producers, traders and consumers, as well as through clearing banks. This underscores the US Dollar's pivotal role as the backbone of global trade and its deep entrenchment in the mechanics of international financial systems.

Financial markets specialising in foreign currency trading play a crucial role in determining exchange rates between currencies, particularly in relation to the USD. These markets provide a platform where participants engage in key activities:
- ✓ **Trading:** *facilitating active buy-sell transactions that drive price discovery.*
- ✓ **Liquidity:** *availability of a continuous flow of buyers and sellers, enabling seamless transactions.*
- ✓ **Hedging:** *allowing market participants to manage and transfer risk through transactions of financial instruments.*

The interplay of these activities, ***trading, liquidity*** and ***hedging*** supports the stability of the global financial system. This stability is vital for the smooth and transparent functioning of international trade, ensuring efficient capital flows between countries.

The ***U.S. Fixed-Income Bond Markets*** offer access to a wide range of debt securities, including U.S. Treasuries (USTs), Mortgage-Backed Securities (MBSs), Commercial Bonds (CBs) and Private Debt. see [Box 1A] These markets are the largest and most liquid globally, ***liquidity*** being the financial term for assets that are actively traded with a consistent availability of buyers and sellers.

These financial instruments play a crucial role in international finance, allowing countries to buy and sell fixed-income securities as part of their foreign reserves management. The unparalleled liquidity and depth of these markets make them a cornerstone of global financial stability and a preferred choice for central banks and institutional investors.

> [Box 1A] A **bond** is a **"financial instrument"** or **"security"** representing a loan or debt, where the borrower agrees to pay accrued interest (referred to as the **"coupon"**) periodically based on the bond's face value (the "notional" or "principal"). The principal is repaid at a pre-agreed end date, known as the "maturity". Typically, bonds pay a fixed coupon at regular intervals (usually every six months) until maturity, when the notional amount is redeemed.
>
> If the borrower is the U.S. government, the bond is referred to as **"U.S. Treasuries"**. If the borrower is a private entity under a private arrangement, the loan is termed **"Private Debt"**. If the borrower is a commercial entity, then it is categorised as a **"Commercial Bond"**. If the bond's coupon payments and notional value are derived from a pool of mortgages, it is known as a **"Mortgage-Backed Security"**.
>
> These bonds, along with many other debt-related instruments, are collectively known as **"Fixed-Income Securities"**. USD-denominated bonds are among the most liquid and tradeable assets, available almost around the clock, 24 hours a day, five days a week, accessible across global markets from Asia to Europe to the United States.

If Country A buys more from Country B than it sells back to Country B, it may struggle to generate enough revenue to pay for its current and future purchases. In this situation, Country A would need to borrow from Country B or other sources to finance its needs. This imbalance between imports and exports is known as a **"Trade Imbalance"**, a commonly referenced economic indicator.

Trade imbalances are considered problematic by international trading partners because they create frictions that can often escalate into conflicts. These imbalances can strain economic relations and lead to tensions over issues like debt, currency exchange and trade policies.

The British fought two Opium Wars with China, primarily driven by trade imbalances. At the time, the British were importing large quantities of goods such as tea and silk from China but struggled to generate enough revenue to pay for them. In response, the British began selling opium to the Chinese, allowing them to fund their purchases of sought-after Chinese goods. Despite the Chinese government's objections to the opium trade, unscrupulous British merchants, often supported by the British Navy, continued to smuggle the drug into China.

The tensions between the two sides eventually escalated into two conflicts, the Opium Wars, fought between 1839 and 1860. The wars left the Chinese economy in ruins and contributed to the downfall of the Qing Dynasty. The emperor fled to Manchuria, leaving behind a weakened army and government. In the aftermath, China was forced to concede additional trading rights and port access to the British.

One of the significant outcomes was the cession of Hong Kong (including Hong Kong Island and the New Territories) to the British under a 150-year lease, which lasted until July 1, 1997, the official handover date. [5]

In the early 1980s, the United States experienced a trade deficit, a situation where the U.S. spent more than it earned, resulting in a net negative trade position. This imbalance pressured countries like Germany and Japan to allow their currencies to appreciate (or strengthen) against the USD. In 1985, the ***Plaza Accord*** was established, calling for a controlled depreciation of the U.S. dollar against the major world currencies.

Among the affected currencies, the Japanese yen (JPY) shouldered the largest burden by appreciating the most against the USD. This move was partly in response to the U.S.-Japan trade deficit, where Japan was exporting more to the U.S. than it was importing. A weaker USD relative to the JPY made U.S. imports into Japan cheaper, enhancing their competitiveness. As a result, Japan increased its imports from the U.S., helping to balance the trade deficit.

However, the sharp appreciation of the JPY forced the Bank of Japan (BOJ) to respond with aggressive monetary easing, which included large and rapid interest rate cuts. This led to lax lending practices, fuelling a speculative bubble in both the stock market and real estate.

When the BOJ attempted to curb these speculative excesses by raising interest rates again, the market reacted negatively, triggering panic. The situation worsened with the U.S. imposing higher tariffs on Japanese exports in an attempt to reduce the trade deficit further. This intensified the economic strain, causing Japan's economy to falter. The speculative bubble ultimately burst, leading to a prolonged period of deflation that persisted until the mid-2020s.

Despite substantial monetary stimulus programs by the BOJ, Japan's lost decades remain largely unrecovered, with lingering effects of deflation and economic stagnation, even as some vestiges of inflation have reappeared in mid-2024. [6]

During my time working in Tokyo in 1997, I recall that a bowl of ramen at Tokyo Station cost JPY 700. When I visited again in 2016, the price of the same bowl of ramen was still around JPY 700! In contrast, a bowl of fishball noodles in Singapore cost SGD 2 in 1997, but by 2016, the price had risen to SGD 3.50 for the same dish from the same stall.

This presents a tale of two cities: deflation in Japan and inflation in Singapore. While property prices in Japan in 2024 have yet to recover to the levels seen during the 1980s, those in Singapore have soared during the same period. This is how deflation and inflation manifest in the everyday lives of people, the battle of ramen vs fishball noodles!

In subsequent chapters, we will explore how both deflation and inflation, when excessive, can be detrimental to the economy.

USD SETTLEMENT MECHANISM

All trades denominated in USD must be settled within a settlement platform which has two components:
SWIFT and *Clearing Banks*.
(SWIFT stands for Society for Worldwide Interbank Financial Telecommunication)

SWIFT is a secure messaging network *(like WhatsApp)* used by banks and financial institutions worldwide to communicate and exchange payment instructions. Through SWIFT, financial institutions send and receive information related to financial transactions in a secure, standardised and reliable manner.

With its extensive global reach, SWIFT connects over 11,000 financial institutions in more than 200 countries, making it the backbone of international financial messaging, including for USD transactions. SWIFT ensures all messages are executed securely and in a standardised format, which helps minimise errors in cross-border transactions.

SWIFT provides a standardised message format (*such as MT103 for international wire transfers*) that allows banks to exchange payment instructions, whether it's a request for a fund transfer or a confirmation of settlement. While SWIFT facilitates communication between banks, it does not move the money itself, the actual transfer of funds is handled by clearing banks. [Study Notes 1]

Clearing banks play a crucial role in the movement of money within the **USD clearing system**. These banks act as intermediaries that settle payments between institutions. Major U.S. banks often serve as clearing banks for USD transactions because they hold accounts with the **Federal Reserve**, which is the U.S. central bank, enabling them to clear payments denominated in USD. Clearing banks facilitate the transfer of funds between the *sending bank* (*the bank initiating the transaction*) and the *receiving bank* (*the bank receiving the funds*).

When a foreign bank wants to send USD to another bank, it typically routes the transaction through a U.S. clearing bank that has access to the **Federal Reserve System**. For foreign banks without direct access to the Federal Reserve, they maintain **correspondent accounts** with U.S. clearing banks. These U.S. clearing banks act on behalf of foreign banks, helping them facilitate USD transactions. This process is known as *correspondent banking*.

Within United States, USD payments are typically settled through one of two systems:

Fedwire: operated by the Federal Reserve, it is a real-time settlement system used for large-value USD payments.

CHIPS (Clearing House Interbank Payments System): a privately operated system that facilitates USD payments between major global financial institutions, managing large volume of cross-border payments.

In correspondent banking, banks maintain accounts with one another. A European bank's USD account held in a U.S. clearing bank is called a Nostro account.

Five Steps in a typical USD Clearing Transaction

Step 1	A bank in Germany *(say Bayerische Landesbank, "**BLB**")* wants to send USD 1 million to a supplier in the U.S., whose account is at a U.S. bank *(say J.P. Morgan, "**JPM**")*.
Step 2	**BLB** doesn't have direct access to the U.S. financial system, so it has a ***Nostro*** account in a U.S. clearing bank *(say Bank of New York Mellon, "**BNY**")*.
Step 3	**BLB** sends a SWIFT message *(MT103)* to **BNY**, instructing it to debit **BLB**'s ***Nostro*** account and credit **JPM**'s account, favouring the U.S. Supplier, whose account at **JPM** is also provided.
Step 4	**BNY** debits **BLB**'s ***Nostro*** account and credits **JPM**'s account at the Federal Reserve via Fedwire or CHIPS.
Step 5	**JPM** then credits the supplier's account, completing the transaction.

When you someday, stand at the bank counter filling up a form to do a telegraphic transfer of USD to some overseas party, the terms Clearing Bank, Swift Code, CHIPS

Number and Correspondent Bank, you will know by then, are part of Fives Steps of USD clearing transaction as described.

The settlement of international cross-border USD payments must be cleared by clearing banks, which ensure that payments are properly settled in USD. They do this through either real-time settlement (*via Fedwire*) or settlement (*via CHIPS*). Clearing banks help manage liquidity in the system by ensuring the smooth settlement of large-value payments. They also assume some degree of counterparty risk by acting as intermediaries in these transactions.

U.S. clearing banks are subject to U.S. financial regulations, including *anti-money laundering (AML)* laws and sanctions imposed by the U.S. government. As a result, even international payments involving USD can be subject to U.S. regulatory scrutiny. Clearing banks must comply with these regulations and sanction directives, or they risk facing severe consequences, akin to the wrath of Darth Vader in Star Wars!

UNITED STATES AND USD DOMINANCE

The combination of the SWIFT network and U.S. clearing banks, much like a horse and carriage team working in tandem, means that the U.S. has significant control over global USD-denominated transactions. Even payments between two foreign countries in USD often pass through U.S.-based clearing banks, granting the U.S. authority over those transactions, particularly in enforcing sanctions or financial restrictions. The reliance on SWIFT and U.S. clearing banks creates challenges for other countries and institutions. Entities that oppose U.S. interests, such as Iran, Russia and Venezuela, have faced sanction risks because of this system.

In response, countries like China and Russia have developed alternative systems to SWIFT, such as China's *CIPS (Cross-Border Interbank Payment System)*, to reduce their reliance on SWIFT for international trade and to mitigate sanctions risk.

The ***USD Settlement Mechanism***, supported by SWIFT and clearing banks, forms the backbone of international USD transactions. SWIFT provides the secure messaging infrastructure, while clearing banks handle the actual settlement of funds. Together, they ensure the efficient and secure transfer of USD globally, with clearing banks playing a crucial role in connecting foreign banks to the U.S. financial system. This controlled efficiency and convenience have given the U.S. considerable influence over global finance.

The USD continued to gain widespread acceptance in international trade. After World War II, the United States was able to demonstrate leadership in *Three Main Pillars*, which contributed to the USD's widespread use as a reference currency.

FIRST PILLAR: POLITICAL LEADERSHIP

The United States has long been recognised for its political leadership on the world stage. U.S. leaders have consistently broken new ground in global politics, a trend that continues to this day. This political leadership played a crucial role in the rise of the USD as a widely accepted reference currency, which many countries adopted for international trade and reserves management.

One prominent example is ***President Richard Nixon***, who, despite resigning in 1974 because of the Watergate scandal, is credited with establishing better diplomatic relations with the People's Republic of China. Nixon's National Security Adviser, ***Henry***

Kissinger, engaged in many talks with Chinese Premier ***Zhou Enlai*** in 1971, setting the stage for a historic shift in U.S.-China relations. In February 1972, Nixon became the first U.S. president to visit China, and during this visit, the ***Shanghai Communiqué*** was issued, articulating the *"One China Principle."*

This diplomatic breakthrough began with what became known as *"Ping-pong Diplomacy"*. At the 1971 World Table Tennis Championships in Nagoya, Japan, a conversation between an American and a Chinese table tennis player led to an invitation for the U.S. team to visit China, followed by a reciprocal invitation. This exchange catalysed a major shift in relations between the two nations.

Nixon's subsequent visit to China resulted in the normalisation of diplomatic relations in 1979, marking a significant turning point in the Cold War. It effectively created an ideological rift between the ***Soviet Union*** and ***China***, leading to Soviet concessions and ultimately contributing to the Soviet Union's collapse. The positive effects of Nixon's visit continue to be felt today, as diplomatic engagement between the U.S. and China remains a central component of global politics, despite fluctuations in their relationship. [7]

SECOND PILLAR: ECONOMIC LEADERSHIP

The economic power of the United States has been unmatched for much of modern history. Even though its Gross Domestic Product (GDP) growth rate has slowed in recent years, it remains a dominant force in the global economy. ***During the 1980s***, under **President Ronald Reagan**, the U.S. economy experienced significant growth, averaging a GDP growth of 3.48% per year. This period was marked by tight monetary policy implemented by Federal Reserve Chairman ***Paul Volcker***, who raised interest rates to historic highs in an effort to curb inflation. While this led to an initial contraction of the economy, it ultimately resulted in a strong economic rebound.

"Reaganomics" was characterised by government downsizing, tax cuts, deregulation and an increased defence budget, all of which led to higher government deficits but also sparked economic growth. The period from ***1990 to 1999*** saw one of the longest periods of peacetime economic expansion in history, with an average GDP growth of 3.58% per annum. [8] This era was marked by low inflation, a booming stock market and significant productivity gains, largely driven by the ***technology boom***, particularly in software, hardware and the internet sectors.

In 1995, the creation of the ***World Trade Organization (WTO)*** further spurred global economic growth by promoting trade liberalisation and reducing barriers to international commerce.

During ***Bill Clinton's*** **presidency** *(1993-2001)*, the U.S. experienced economic prosperity, including trade surpluses. The U.S. began exporting more goods and services than it imported, resulting in a positive trade balance. This period of growth was also facilitated by the ratification of the ***North American Free Trade Agreement (NAFTA)*** in ***January 1994***, which created a free trade bloc between the U.S., Canada and Mexico. NAFTA boosted economic growth on the North American continent by increasing trade and investment flows. ***In 2020***, NAFTA was replaced by *the* ***United States-Mexico-Canada Agreement (USMCA)*** under the Trump administration, which aimed to strengthen the trade relations among the three nations. [9]

THIRD PILLAR: MILITARY LEADERSHIP

The moment the United States dropped atomic bombs Little Boy and Fat Man on Hiroshima and Nagasaki on August 6th and 9th, 1945, the world entered the nuclear age. These two bombs, using fission technology, released massive amounts of energy by splitting uranium (in Little Boy) and plutonium (in Fat Man) atoms. This pivotal moment marked the beginning of *U.S. military dominance* on the global stage, as it showed not only technological advancement but also unparalleled military capability. [10]

From the *Vietnam War* in the 1960s and early 1970s to the *invasions of Afghanistan (2001)* and *Iraq (2003)*, the United States repeatedly showcased its military superiority. The combination of agile armoured vehicles, advanced weaponry, precision-guided smart bombs, cutting-edge fighter jets and high-tech surveillance systems transformed the U.S. military into a formidable force capable of defeating any potential aggressor. The *nuclear-powered aircraft carrier fleet* patrolling the high seas ensured that the U.S. maintained *naval supremacy*, extending its global reach.

This overwhelming military dominance gave the world a sense of security and stability, as the U.S. was perceived as a guarantor of free and unrestricted access for vessels, both in the air, at sea and on land, essential for facilitating international trade. Through this military prowess, the U.S. effectively positioned itself as the global "policeman," upholding law and order on the world stage, ensuring safe and secure trade routes, and asserting influence over global geopolitics.

THREE PILLARS OF INFLUENCE

The *Three Pillars of Influence: Political, Economic* and *Military*, collectively known as *PoEM*, established by the *United States of America*, played a crucial role in solidifying the *USD* as the preferred currency for international commerce and as a standard for investment denomination.

These three pillars gave holders of *USD-denominated assets* confidence in the preservation of value, ensuring that the USD remained the primary medium of exchange and a trusted currency for investments globally. The *PoEM framework* not only underpinned the economic dominance of the U.S. but also fostered international reliance on the USD, cementing its role as the currency of choice in the global financial system.

TRADE IMPACT OF USD DOMINANCE

The USD's unparalleled role in international trade and global finance is rooted in several critical factors that make it the cornerstone of global economic activity.

Perception of Stability: the USD benefits from the political, economic and military stability of the United States, which reassures investors and institutions. Its status as a safe-haven currency means it is a preferred choice during economic downturns or geopolitical crises, offering a reliable store of value.

Liquidity and Accessibility: the USD is highly liquid, supported by deep financial markets, particularly in fixed-income and foreign-exchange sectors. Its accessibility ensures that global traders and investors can transact seamlessly, enhancing its role as a trusted medium of exchange.

Global Trade Currency: many commodities, including oil, gold, and iron ore, are universally priced in USD. This standardisation compels buyers and sellers worldwide to transact in USD, reinforcing its centrality in global trade. Even in transactions between non-U.S. entities, the USD is frequently chosen for its stability and ease of use. For instance, a Turkish company trading with a South Korean firm may price transactions in USD to avoid risks associated with fluctuating local currencies.

Confidence in Value Preservation: the USD's position as a reserve currency instils confidence in its value stability, making it a preferred asset during times of uncertainty. Predictable U.S. monetary policy and robust economic fundamentals further solidify this confidence among central banks and global investors.

Simplification of Transactions: by invoicing in USD, companies minimise transaction risks associated with volatile exchange rates, ensuring predictable pricing for long-term agreements. Using the USD streamlines international trade by eliminating the need for cumbersome currency conversions, especially for weaker or less stable currencies.

Minimisation of Exchange Rate Risk: the USD's use as a universal trade currency mitigates exchange rate risks, reducing volatility and uncertainty in cross-border transactions.

Widespread Acceptance: as the most globally accepted currency, the USD ensures smooth and efficient execution of payments across borders. Its universal trust and credibility allow it to function as the linchpin of global commerce, fostering economic stability.

Reserve Currency Status: the USD is the most widely held reserve currency globally, with central banks allocating significant portions of their foreign exchange reserves in USD. This preference stems from the USD's stability, reliability and global acceptance, making it a vital tool for safeguarding reserves and managing international liquidity.

The USD's dominance is more than a financial phenomenon, it is a structural feature of the global economic system. Its role in commodity pricing, widespread acceptability and inherent stability not only simplify international trade but also enable efficient and secure market operations. The USD's entrenched position underscores its ability to shape trade patterns, influence global economic policies and sustain confidence in international markets.

THE PETRODOLLAR SYSTEM AND ITS EVOLUTION

The ***Petrodollar system*** has been a cornerstone of global trade since its establishment in the 1970s, ensuring the USD's dominance in international finance and bolstering U.S. economic influence. However, recent developments, particularly involving China, suggest the system may face significant challenges, potentially ushering in a new era of ***"PetroRMB"*** transactions.

Understanding the Petrodollar System: the Petrodollar System emerged when oil-exporting countries agreed to price and transact oil exclusively in USD. This system was supported by agreements between the U.S. and major oil producers, particularly Saudi Arabia and OPEC nations, ensuring a steady demand for USD globally. Countries importing oil needed to hold USD reserves to pay for their energy imports, creating a cycle that reinforced the dollar's position as the world's dominant currency. As a result, oil exporters accumulated vast USD reserves, which they reinvested in U.S. financial markets, supporting liquidity and funding U.S. deficits.

Shifts in Global Energy Trade: to disrupt this Petrodollar System, China has made some strategic moves. At the China-GCC Summit in 2022, President Xi Jinping encouraged **Gulf Cooperation Council (GCC)** states to utilise the Shanghai Petroleum and National Gas Exchange for oil and gas trades settled in RMB. China is one of the largest importers of GCC oil, providing a strong economic rationale for RMB-denominated transactions. Agreements were made to increase collaboration in LNG imports, upstream development and energy logistics, further solidifying China's role as a major energy partner for the GCC. If RMB settlement becomes widespread, it could weaken the USD's grip on global oil trade, shifting power dynamics in international finance.

U.S. Energy Independence: in 2022, the U.S. transitioned to become a net energy exporter, significantly reducing its reliance on Middle Eastern oil supplies. This shift undermines the original geopolitical foundations of the Petrodollar system, which relied on strong U.S.-Saudi ties to maintain the USD's dominance. With reduced dependence on OPEC and Saudi Arabia, both Saudi Arabia and the U.S. have less incentive to uphold the traditional Petrodollar system.

Potential for a PetroRMB System: the growing prominence of the RMB as an alternative to the USD reflects broader shifts in global economic power. If major oil exporters, particularly GCC states, adopt RMB settlement, it could significantly weaken the demand for USD in global markets. However, there are challenges to RMB adoption. The RMB is still not fully convertible, and China's financial markets lack the depth and transparency of U.S. markets. Many countries remain cautious about over-reliance on China's currency due to potential political and economic risks.

Implications for Global Finance: the PetroRMB is a threat to USD hegemony. A shift from Petrodollar to PetroRMB transactions would reduce global reliance on the USD, potentially destabilising its role as the primary reserve currency. The decline of the Petrodollar system could lead to a redistribution of economic influence, with China and other emerging economies gaining greater control over global trade patterns. Geopolitical realignment of interests amongst countries would be inevitable. As the demand for USD decreases, the U.S. may face challenges in funding deficits and maintaining liquidity in its financial markets.

The Petrodollar system has long been a pillar of the USD's global dominance, but evolving energy markets and geopolitical dynamics pose a significant challenge. While the Petrodollar's relevance may diminish, its potential replacement by a PetroRMB system will depend on China's ability to build trust in its currency and financial markets. For now, the world watches as these economic and geopolitical shifts unfold, heralding a potential transformation in the landscape of global trade and finance.

USD IN INTERNATIONAL FINANCE

The USD plays a pivotal role in international debt issuance and global payment systems, reinforcing its dominance in global trade and finance. Over half of all international loans and bonds are denominated in USD, as developing countries like India, Vietnam and South Africa often prefer to borrow in USD. This preference is driven by lower U.S. interest rates and the high liquidity of U.S. securities compared to their domestic options. However, this comes at the cost of exposure to exchange rate risks, as a weakening local currency against the USD can sharply increase the burden of servicing USD-denominated debt.

A historical example of this vulnerability is the *1997 Asian Financial Crisis*, where the collapse of Thailand's pegged exchange rate triggered currency devaluations across the region, including the Korean Won, Malaysian Ringgit and Indonesian Rupiah, escalating debt pressures and deepening the crisis. [11]

The USD's dominance is further cemented by its central role in global payment systems like SWIFT, where a significant share of transactions is settled in USD. U.S. clearing banks, operating through systems like Fedwire and CHIPS, ensure the smooth settlement of USD payments worldwide. These systems not only simplify international trade but also underscore the USD's global importance.

While the USD's stability, liquidity and global acceptance make it a preferred currency for borrowing and trade, this dominance also presents challenges for developing economies. They benefit from access to international capital but remain vulnerable to currency risks, U.S. monetary policy shifts and dependency on USD-centric payment frameworks.

The influence of U.S. monetary policy on global markets is profound, largely due to the USD's dominant role in international trade and finance. The Federal Reserve's decisions on interest rates significantly impact the global economy. When the Fed raises interest rates, the USD strengthens, making U.S. exports costlier and imports cheaper. This can suppress global demand for U.S. goods while benefiting foreign exporters. Conversely, when rates are lowered, the USD weakens, bolstering U.S. exports but increasing import costs for American consumers, thereby shifting trade balances.

The Federal Reserve also plays a crucial role in ensuring global financial stability through USD liquidity. During financial crises, many nations depend on the *Fed's swap lines;* pre-agreed arrangements that allow foreign central banks to access USD liquidity in exchange for their own currencies or assets. *These swap lines act as a financial safety net, helping stabilise economies facing sudden dollar shortages, much like a "big brother" offering critical support during turbulent times.*

The USD's dominance extends to the global foreign-exchange (Forex) market, where it serves as the anchor currency. It is involved in nearly 90% of all Forex transactions, making it a benchmark for global currency valuations. The daily Forex traded volume globally is estimated to be around USD 5 trillion. Many countries peg their currencies to the USD or manage exchange rates relative to it, further entrenching the USD's influence. These interconnected factors ensure that U.S. monetary policy decisions ripple across global markets, influencing trade, investment flows and economic stability worldwide.

Currency pegs fix the exchange rate of a country's currency to a reference currency, often the USD, for stability in trade and economic management. This system is commonly used in regions such as the Middle East and Asia, where economies like Saudi Arabia and Hong Kong have adopted USD pegs. By anchoring their currencies to the USD, these countries benefit from stabilised pricing of goods and services and seamless access to the USD settlement mechanism for international trade transactions. However, this also links their monetary policies directly to U.S. interest rates.

Hong Kong has pegged its currency, the Hong Kong Dollar (HKD), to the USD within a tight band of HKD 7.75 to 7.85 since October 1983. Despite challenges from currency speculators during financial crises, this peg remains intact, supported by Hong Kong's autonomy as a Special Administrative Region (SAR) of China, which allows it to maintain its own currency until 2047.

The peg, while stabilising the exchange rate, has implications for Hong Kong's economy. A weaker USD raises the cost of imports from non-USD regions, fuelling inflationary pressures in Hong Kong, which relies heavily on imported goods and consumables. Conversely, a stronger USD increases the cost of visiting Hong Kong for tourists from other regions, potentially reducing its attractiveness as a tourist destination. This dynamic makes Hong Kong's economy vulnerable to fluctuations in the USD, underscoring the trade-offs inherent in a pegged currency system.

The USD's dominance in global trade and finance grants the U.S. extraordinary geopolitical influence through the power to impose economic sanctions. Because most international transactions involve the USD and are processed through U.S.-based clearing banks, the U.S. can effectively deny access to the global financial system for countries, organisations or individuals that contravene its policies. This ability to restrict access has been a potent tool in enforcing sanctions, as seen in cases like Iran and Russia, where sanctions have curtailed these nations' participation in international trade and markets.

However, this leverage has also motivated countries to explore alternatives to the USD-centric system. Concerns over dependency on the USD settlement mechanism and the risk of being excluded from global financial networks have spurred efforts to reduce reliance on the U.S. Dollar. Initiatives such as promoting local currency trade agreements and developing alternative payment systems aim to diversify international trade away from USD hegemony, reflecting a broader strategy to mitigate the influence of U.S. financial and geopolitical policies.

China is actively working to elevate the RMB in international trade through strategies like bilateral trade agreements and the expansive Belt and Road Initiative (BRI). These efforts aim to establish the RMB as a viable alternative to the USD. Furthermore, China's development of the Cross-Border Interbank Payment System (CIPS) is a deliberate step to reduce dependence on the SWIFT network for global transactions, enhancing the RMB's appeal in cross-border payments.

In addition, the rise of digital currencies, including cryptocurrencies and central bank digital currencies (CBDCs), presents another potential challenge to USD dominance. For instance, China's Digital Yuan is positioned as a contender in the evolving landscape of digital financial ecosystems. These initiatives are gradually creating avenues for countries to diversify away from the USD-centric trade and financial systems.

Despite these advancements, the USD remains the predominant currency in global trade and finance. Its unparalleled liquidity, stability, vast trade volumes and widespread acceptance ensure its continued centrality in the international monetary system. While challenges to its dominance are emerging, the USD's entrenched role as the world's leading currency endures for now.

USD IS EVERYWHERE

The Three Pillars of Influence, **Political, Economic,** and **Military (PoEM),** solidify the global presence of the United States, with impacts felt across political broadcasts, commercial expansion and military reach. U.S. political involvement often dominates global headlines, as evidenced by events like live coverage of the 47th U.S. Presidential Election in November 2024, which captivated international audiences. The prevalence of U.S. commercial icons like McDonald's, Starbucks, Tesla Apple and Microsoft, coupled with military hardware such as F-16 fighters and Apache helicopters, highlights the extensive reach of U.S. influence in daily life worldwide.

These elements serve as carriers of the USD's prominence. Broadcasting of U.S. politics, the global footprint of U.S. brands and the proliferation of U.S. military technology ensure the ubiquity of the USD. The USD becomes an inseparable companion in the spread of U.S. culture, products and geopolitical presence, riding on the waves of this broad-based influence to establish itself as the default currency for international trade, finance and transactions.

The USD is deeply embedded in the global economy as the *reserve currency*, the primary medium for trade and commodities, and a critical element of international payment systems. The petrodollar system, the issuance of USD-denominated debt and the far-reaching effects of U.S. monetary policy cement its importance. These factors ensure the USD's status as an omnipresent force in international trade and global markets.

While some nations are actively exploring alternatives, including China's RMB and digital currencies, the USD remains unmatched in terms of stability, liquidity and widespread acceptance. For now, and the foreseeable future, ***USD is everywhere***, profoundly shaping the world's economic and financial landscape.

Chapter 2
Exit the British Pound and Enter the U.S. Dollar
The Rise and Fall of the British Pound, Enter the U.S. Dollar, the death of the Gold Standard and the rise of Fiat Currencies...

The USD plays a crucial role in international trade and global finance, underpinned by the influence of three main pillars: ***Political, Economic, and Military (PoEM)***. These pillars worked together over time to build the credibility and global reach of the USD, making it the preferred currency for commodities, goods, services and financial assets. However, the USD did not become the world's de facto reserve currency overnight. Its dominance evolved gradually, shaped by political leadership, economic changes and the development of global financial infrastructure.

For a currency to be considered the ***de facto reserve currency***, it must be widely accepted in international trade and global finance, acting as a reference currency in transactions and a major denomination for reserves held by central banks. While the USD is the primary reserve currency for most countries, sovereign nations typically do not hold 100% of their reserves in a single currency. Diversification of assets is common to mitigate risks and ensure the stability of reserves.

BRITISH POUND AND THE BRITISH EMPIRE

Before the USD ascended to its dominant global status, the British Pound Sterling (GBP) held the position of the world's primary reserve currency during the 18th and 19th centuries. The prominence of the GBP was supported by the same foundational ***"PoEM"*** pillars, ***Political, Economic, and Military*** influence, that later underpinned the rise of the USD.

POLITICAL INFLUENCE
The British Empire's vast colonial reach played a critical role in establishing the GBP as the world's leading currency. At its height, the British Empire spanned nearly a quarter of the globe's population, encompassing territories in the far east, such as India, Hong Kong, Malaysia and Singapore, as well as in the west, including Canada, parts of North America, Australia and even the Falkland Islands.

This expansive empire allowed Britain to spread its political and cultural influence widely, embedding the English language, British customs and governance structures such as the Rule of Law and the Parliamentary System of Government across its colonies. These systems left a lasting legacy, continuing to shape many former colonies even after they gained independence. The political ideology of the empire not only solidified Britain's influence but also established the GBP as the preferred currency within these territories for trade and economic transactions.

The empire's political structure, combined with its ability to project authority across continents, created a foundation of trust and stability in the British financial system, which reinforced the GBP's position as the de facto reserve currency of its time.

ECONOMIC INFLUENCE
The economic dominance of the British Empire, which cemented the GBP as the world's reserve currency, was fuelled significantly by the Industrial Revolution in the

18th century. This transformative period marked the beginning of a new era of technological advancements, economic expansion and global trade dominance for Britain. The Industrial Revolution ushered in a wave of groundbreaking inventions and innovations, many of which were applied on an industrial scale, enabling Britain to become a global economic powerhouse. This newfound economic strength allowed Britain to produce high-value capital goods and export them worldwide, reinforcing the importance of the GBP in international trade.

The Steam Locomotive: recognised as the inventor of the steam railway locomotive in 1803, Richard Trevithick adapted the steam engine which James Watt had invented earlier. The first steam-powered locomotive carried paid passengers from Liverpool to Manchester, designed by English engineer George Stephenson and his son. The locomotive christened the *"Rocket"*, achieved a speed of 36 miles (58 km) per hour, a decent speed during those periods. [1]

Electric Generators and Motors: Michael Faraday, a British Scientist, discovered that by passing an electric current through a coil of wire between two poles of a magnet, it could cause the coil to turn. Conversely, by turning a coil of wire between two poles of a magnet, an electric current in the coil could be generated. The first phenomenon formed the basis of the electric motor, electric generator or dynamo. This eventually led to the introduction of electric railways and tramways. The first electrified section of the London Underground began operation in 1890, from Paddington to Baker Street Station to Farringdon. [2]

Telegraph and Telephone: the first practical electric telegraph systems were created almost simultaneously in Britain and the United States in 1837. Developed by British inventors, the telegraph machine had needles on a mounting plate at a receiver pointing to specific letters or numbers when electric current passed through attached wires. The telephone was invented by Scottish-born American scientist Alexander Grahan Bell. The telephone enabled voice to be transmitted by means of an electric current. [3] Modern telecommunications today, through the travails of Bell and his cohorts, have progressed by leaps and bounds giving rise to fibre-optic cables, hearing aids, wi-fi and the ubiquitous cell phone technology.

With these technological advancements, Britain became the *"workshop of the world"*, exporting industrial goods while importing raw materials from its colonies and trading partners. This dominance in global trade positioned the GBP as the preferred currency for international transactions and a trusted store of value.

Moreover, Britain's robust banking and financial institutions, centered around the City of London, provided the infrastructure for managing international trade and investment. The establishment of systems like the ***gold standard***, which pegged the GBP to gold, further enhanced confidence in the stability and reliability of the currency.

In summary, the economic influence of Britain during the Industrial Revolution played a pivotal role in solidifying the GBP's global supremacy, as it became the medium through which the world engaged in trade and commerce. This period not only elevated Britain's economic stature but also entrenched the GBP as the global reserve and trade currency of its time.

MILITARY INFLUENCE

At its height, Britain's **naval supremacy** allowed it to control key global trade routes and protect its colonies. This military power ensured the security of international trade, boosting confidence in the use of the GBP. Additionally, Britain's **military presence** in strategic ports around the world provided further stability, reinforcing GBP's role in global commerce.

A little digression...here is an interesting historical example of British Naval superiority:

The Battle of Trafalgar, 21st October 1805.
The British Royal Navy fleet of 27 ships led by **Admiral Lord Horatio Nelson** *on the HMS Victory went to battle outnumbered against the Franco-Spanish fleet of 33 led by Vice-Admiral Pierre Villeneuve, off the Spanish coast of Cadiz. Nelson's battle plan emphasised more on the skills and experience of his officers and men, rather than the strength of his ships. His unorthodox battle plan gave him the victory but at the expense of his own life. He was killed by a musket shot which pierced through his left shoulder, smashed two ribs and tore through his left lung, severing a major artery.*

The Battle Statistics: *British Royal Navy Fleet Size of 27 ships versus the Franco-Spanish Fleet Size of 33 ships.* **Post battle** *saw 17 enemy ships captured, four escaped but were captured weeks later. One ship managed to struggle back to Cadiz. The British lost 449 sailors, about ten times less than what was inflicted on the Franco-Spanish navy. The British also took 20,000 prisoners during this epic battle. This Battle reinforced Britain's reputation as ruler of the seas and demonstrated the Royal Navy's superiority in training, professionalism and expertise in naval tactics that set her apart from her rivals.* [4]

The combination of political, economic, and military (PoEM) strength positioned the British pound (GBP) as the preferred global trade and reserve currency during the 18th and 19th centuries. In contrast, Spain and France, with comparatively weaker PoEM pillars, were unable to challenge Britain's dominance. Britain's global economic leadership, expansive empire and sophisticated financial system solidified the British Pound's supremacy as the world's reserve currency well into the early 20th century.

WAR BROKE OUT AND ALL HELL BROKE LOOSE

At the onset of World War I in 1914, Britain suspended the gold standard to prevent a drain on its gold reserves. The Bank of England ceased exchanging paper money for gold to maintain financial stability and fund the war effort. This suspension enabled the government to print money to finance military expenditures without being constrained by gold reserves.

After the war, Britain sought to restore the gold standard at the pre-war parity of the British Pound to the U.S. Dollar. In 1925, under Chancellor Winston Churchill, the gold standard was reinstated. However, this decision proved controversial, as it led to economic difficulties such as deflation and a loss of competitiveness for British exports.

The return to the gold standard ultimately became unsustainable during the economic turmoil of the Great Depression. In 1931, Britain permanently abandoned the gold standard, allowing the British Pound to float and marking the end of its commitment to a fixed gold exchange system. While Britain did not permanently leave the gold standard in 1914, the disruptions of World War I set the stage for its eventual collapse.

ENTER THE UNITED STATES DOLLAR

The classic martial arts movie **Enter the Dragon** featured Bruce Lee taking on formidable adversaries in a high-stakes tournament, ultimately triumphing against the sinister drug lord Han. In a similar vein, the British Pound, once the dominant reserve currency, found itself displaced in the aftermath of two global conflicts. The British Pound's decline mirrored the fate of Han's strongman O'Hara, defeated by a superior opponent.

"Enter the United States Dollar", the metaphorical Bruce Lee of global currencies. The USD emerged as the ultimate victor, securing its place as the world's primary reserve currency following the economic upheavals of World War One and World War Two. Much like Lee's undercover mission to expose Han's operations, the USD's ascendancy was driven by America's economic and military dominance, reshaping the global financial order. While the British Pound's reign came to an end, the USD stepped into the spotlight, wielding the strength and resilience needed to lead the international monetary system.

World War One (WWI), which began in 1914, was largely fuelled by militarism and imperialism. Militarism involved countries aggressively building up their military forces and relying on military action for conflict resolution, while imperialism was driven by nations seeking to expand their territories through colonisation and conquest. After the war, the **Treaty of Versailles** imposed severe reparations on Germany, forcing them to pay large sums to France and Britain. Britain, in turn, used these payments to settle debts with the United States. The harsh terms of the treaty contributed to domestic unrest in Germany, which was exploited by Adolf Hitler and the Nazi Party, fuelling nationalistic sentiments and eventually leading to the rise of Nazi power. [5]

World War Two (WWII) began on 1st September 1939 when Germany invaded Poland from the West, followed by the Soviet Union invading Poland from the East on 17th September 1939. This invasion was preceded by the Nazi-Soviet Non-Aggression Pact signed on 23rd August 1939, where both Hitler and Stalin agreed to divide Eastern Europe between them. The two World Wars left much of Europe in ruin, with countries like Britain, France, Russia, Germany and Italy facing severe financial burdens due to war debts and reparations. Consequently, the British Pound (GBP) lost its status as the world's reserve currency. [6]

The Bretton Woods System (BWS) was established in July 1944 to address the global economic challenges after World War II. Forty-four countries, including the United States, Canada, Western European nations and Australia, agreed to a new monetary framework aimed at stabilising the international economy. Notably, the Soviet Union opted out. Under this system, currencies were pegged to the U.S. Dollar (USD), which was tied to gold at a rate of $35 per ounce for foreign governments and central banks. Each currency was allowed to fluctuate within a narrow 1% band around a fixed exchange rate.

The *International Monetary Fund (IMF)* was created to monitor exchange rates and provide emergency financial assistance to struggling economies, while the *International Bank for Reconstruction and Development (IBRD)*, later part of the World Bank, focused on rebuilding war-torn European infrastructure. The Bretton Woods framework cemented the U.S. Dollar as the global reserve currency, replacing the British Pound (GBP). The U.S. held significant influence, particularly after Britain, heavily indebted from the war, ratified the agreements in December 1945 in exchange for $4.4 billion in U.S. aid to help rebuild its economy. [7]

The **Bretton Woods System** was designed to stabilise global currencies, avoid competitive devaluations and maintain order in the global monetary system. Fixed exchange rates were established for participating countries, all pegged to the USD, while the USD itself was tied to gold. The U.S. controlled roughly two-thirds of the world's gold reserves, which helped maintain confidence in the system. However, by the 1950s, significant issues began to emerge.

By the **1950s**, the U.S. *Balance of Payments (BoP) was in deficit, meaning the U.S. was importing more than it was exporting, leading to an outflow of USD.* As global trade expanded, the demand for USD outpaced the U.S.'s ability to back them with gold. This created mounting pressure on the U.S. to honour its commitment to convert USD into gold, undermining the stability of the Bretton Woods System. This imbalance was exacerbated by growing global trade and an increasing circulation of USD abroad. The U.S. could not export enough to replenish its gold reserves, leading to fears that the U.S. might not be able to meet the USD-Gold convertibility commitment.

In the **1960s**, the situation worsened as international demand for USD continued to rise, but the U.S. could not match this demand with sufficient gold reserves. The *Gold Pool* was created in **1961** as an attempt to defend the USD-Gold peg. The Gold Pool was a consortium of 10 central banks from countries including the United States, the United Kingdom (UK), Germany, and France, whose goal was to manage the price of gold and defend the peg by buying or selling gold as needed.

The Gold Pool worked to keep the price of gold at the agreed-upon level of $35 per ounce by purchasing gold from the market if the price fell below the peg and selling gold if the price exceeded it. This was intended to stabilise gold prices and support the Bretton Woods system. However, by the **late 1960s**, the system began to face increasing strain due to growing doubts about the USD's ability to maintain its peg to gold.

Several key events contributed to the unravelling of the Gold Pool and, ultimately, the collapse of the Bretton Woods System:

1. **Sterling Crisis (1967):** during this period, a combination of factors, including economic difficulties in the U.S., declining confidence in the UK Labour Government and the Six-Day War which resulted in the closure of the Suez Canal, created turmoil in global financial markets. The GBP was devalued by 15%, which led to a surge in demand for gold. Gold prices began rising above the $35 per ounce peg. As the Gold Pool attempted to intervene by selling gold to prevent the price from escalating, it faced significant losses. The Gold Pool's efforts to defend the peg failed as gold prices surged from $35 per ounce to over $40 per ounce. This exposed the weaknesses in the Bretton Woods framework.

2. **Depletion of Gold Reserves:** the Gold Pool's efforts to sell gold to keep the price down increasingly drained the reserves of participating countries, particularly the U.S., which had to contribute the largest share of the sales. This situation created a two-tier gold market, where countries could buy gold at the fixed price of $35 per ounce, but

could sell it at higher prices on the open market. This undermined the ability of the U.S. to maintain its gold reserves at the levels needed to back the circulating dollars.

3. **Loss of Confidence:** the Gold Pool's collapse was also influenced by declining confidence in the USD. Speculation surrounding the USD's future began to increase, especially as the U.S. was running a growing Balance of Payments deficits and continuing to print more USD. **The Triffin Dilemma** [8], a paradox where the U.S. had to run deficits to provide global liquidity but these deficits eroded confidence in the dollar, put future pressure on the system.

As the Gold Pool failed to stabilise the price of gold, the U.S. was forced to sell more gold than it had in reserves, depleting its gold stockpile. The increasing gold price and dwindling gold reserves exposed the fundamental flaws in the Bretton Woods framework. By **1971**, after several failed attempts to defend the gold standard, U.S. President Richard Nixon made the pivotal decision to suspend the convertibility of the USD into gold. This marked the effective end of the Bretton Woods System and the USD-Gold peg.

Following this suspension, the price of gold skyrocketed as the market realised that the U.S. no longer had sufficient gold reserves to back the global supply of dollars. This shift marked a fundamental transformation in the international monetary system, transitioning from a gold-backed currency system to a fiat currency system, where the value of currency was no longer tied to a physical commodity like gold.

In **1973**, countries within the European Economic Community (EEC) and Japan began to float their currencies, abandoning the fixed exchange rates that had defined the Bretton Woods system. This further undermined the stability of the fixed exchange rate system.

Finally, in **1976**, the Jamaica Accords formally ended the Bretton Woods System by abandoning the gold standard and establishing a system of floating exchange rates for major currencies. This shift marked the end of the USD-Gold Standard and solidified the USD's role as a fiat currency. It also marked the transition to a global monetary system with floating exchange rates. [9]

The collapse of the Bretton Woods System was ultimately the result of several key factors: *growing U.S. Balance of Payments deficits, the Triffin Dilemma, the growing circulation of U.S. Dollars abroad without sufficient gold reserves and the failure of the Gold Pool to defend the USD-Gold peg*. This led to the end of the gold standard and the emergence of the fiat currency system that governs international monetary relations today.

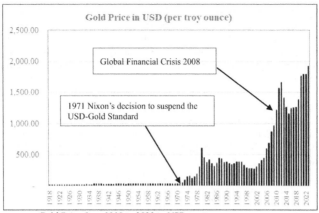

Gold Price from 1918 to 2022 in USD per troy ounce
Source: World Gold Council
Figure 2a: *Post Bretton Woods saw the USD devaluing against Gold up to this present day.*

Covert Currency Reserve Management and Undercover Gold Operations

In the 1960s, both Malaysia and Singapore, as former British colonies, maintained most of their currency reserves in the British Pound (GBP), adhering to a *Minimum Sterling Proportion (MSP)* as part of their commitments to the Commonwealth. However, the economic and political changes of the decade, coupled with Britain's financial instability, led both nations to question their reliance on Sterling reserves.

The split between Singapore and Malaysia in August 1965, marking their paths as independent nations, intensified these considerations. Each country now had greater autonomy over its monetary policy, and the prospect of Sterling's weakening value incentivised diversification. Singapore's Finance Minister, Dr. Goh Keng Swee, anticipating potential risks acted decisively and covertly by reducing Singapore's Sterling reserves from 74% in June 1967 to 50% by October 1967.

Meanwhile, Malaysia's Finance Minister, Tan Siew Sin, took a more cautious approach. Reassured by the British Chancellor in June 1967 that Sterling devaluation was unlikely, Malaysia reduced its Sterling reserves more modestly, from 92% to 82% by October 1967. However, Britain's decision to devalue the Sterling by 14.3% in November 1967 caught Malaysia off guard. Singapore's strategic foresight, coupled with British tolerance of its covert moves, limited its exposure to the devaluation, whereas Malaysia faced more significant financial repercussions.

This episode highlighted Singapore's proactive financial strategy under Goh's leadership, which contrasted with Malaysia's reliance on assurances from Britain. It also strained relations between the two neighbours, as Malaysia perceived Singapore's manoeuvre as a breach of mutual understanding, made more contentious by Singapore's relatively lighter impact from the Sterling devaluation.

At the same time, possibly aware of the fragility of the Bretton Woods System and the potential risks of holding large amounts of Sterling, Dr. Goh took another significant step. In 1968, together with his aide Ngiam Tong Dow, he secretly negotiated the purchase of

100 tons of gold from South Africa at the price of around $40 per troy ounce, above the then-official USD-Gold peg of $35 per ounce. This move, while covert, was a prudent decision that would prove highly profitable once the U.S. abandoned the gold standard. After the USD-Gold peg was abandoned in 1971, gold prices surged, reaching an average of $193 per ounce by 1978 and $615 by 1980, a fifteen-fold increase from the original purchase price.

This gold purchase would go down in history as a remarkably successful investment, akin to the type of trades made by modern-day stellar hedge fund managers. For Dr. Goh, however, it was likely seen as a careful exercise in financial prudence, ensuring that Singapore's reserves were diversified and secure in the face of global instability. The decision to gradually move away from Sterling and diversify into gold proved to be both visionary and fortuitous, cushioning Singapore from the risks of the fluctuating global monetary system and setting them on a more stable financial path.

Professor Catherine Schenk, Professor of Economic and Social History at St Hilda's College, University of Oxford, has documented these pivotal moments in her work, describing in detail how Malaysia and Singapore strategically disentangled themselves from their reliance on Sterling during the final years of the Bretton Woods era, setting the stage for their more diversified and resilient financial strategies in the following decades. [Study Notes 2]

RISE AND FALL OF FIAT CURRENCIES

In 1973, several European Economic Community (EEC) countries and Japan transitioned to a floating exchange rate system, moving away from the fixed exchange rates established by the Bretton Woods Agreement. This shift ended the system where currencies were pegged to the USD, which in turn was linked to gold at a fixed rate of USD35 per ounce. As a result, the USD was no longer tied to gold, leading to its depreciation against many other major currencies and also gold.

This period marked the rise of *fiat currencies*. Fiat currencies are those that do not have intrinsic value or are backed by a physical commodity, like gold or silver. Instead, their value comes solely from the government decree that they are legal tender, meaning they must be accepted as a means of exchange or as a store of value within that country. Essentially, fiat money derives its value from trust in the issuing government and its ability to maintain the stability of the currency, rather than from any tangible asset backing it.
"Fiat currency is backed by government resources, not physical assets like gold" [10]

In a floating exchange rate system, currency values fluctuate based on market forces, such as supply and demand rather than being fixed by an external standard like gold. This shift allowed for more flexible monetary policies but also introduced new risks, such as inflation and currency instability.

Year	Deutsche Mark	Japanese Yen	British Pound	Aussie Dollar
1950	4.1950	361.10	0.3571	0.8929
1961	4.0333	360.00	0.3571	0.8929
1970	3.6600	360.00	0.4166	0.8928
1978	2.0086	210.44	0.5212	0.8737
EURO				
2024	0.9174	150.00	0.7752	1.5152
Source: IMF				
All quoted a units of currency per USD				

Historical Currency Exchange Rates
(* in Jan 1999 the single currency EURO was introduced and so Deutsche Mark was no longer in existence after 1999) [11]

By 1978, the USD had already started depreciating against several key currencies, and this trend continued over the years. By 2024, the value of currencies relative to the USD had evolved significantly:

Japanese Yen: in 1978, one USD was worth about JPY210. Over the decades, Japan's economy grew, and the JPY appreciated. By 2024, the JPY had strengthened by around 30%, with the exchange rate at approximately JPY150 per USD. This reflected Japan's rising economic power.

British Pound: the exchange rate in 1978 was around USD1.92 per GBP. By 2024, the Pound had depreciated by about 33%, with the rate moving to USD1.29 per GBP. This decline was influenced by inflation, the economic impact of Brexit and slower growth in the UK compared to the U.S.

Australian Dollar: in 1978, the exchange rate was USD1.14 per AUD. By 2024, the Australian Dollar had depreciated by around 40%, with the rate at USD0.66 per AUD. This reflected global commodity price fluctuations and shifts in Australia's economic policies.

Overall, the USD has strengthened against the GBP and AUD over the years, reflecting the relative stability of the U.S. economy. However, the JPY has appreciated, marking Japan's increasing influence in the global economy. These changes highlight how global economic shifts and monetary policies under the floating exchange rate system have shaped currency values since the end of the Bretton Woods framework.

FALL OF A FIAT CURRENCY

During the Japanese Occupation of Singapore from 1942 to 1945, the Japanese issued their own currency for use in the territories under their control, including Singapore. These notes, which featured motifs of banana plants, became known as *"Banana Notes"*. Despite being declared legal tender by the Japanese authorities, these notes were effectively fiat money, currency with value based on government decree rather than any intrinsic commodity like gold.

The value of these *"Banana Notes"* was solely supported by the authority of the Japanese military administration. However, when the Japanese Empire fell at the end of World War II, the Japanese governing body in Singapore ceased to exist, and so did the legitimacy of the *"Banana Notes"*. As a result, the currency quickly became worthless, serving as an example of the vulnerabilities inherent in fiat money systems where the value of the currency is dependent on the continued trust in and authority of the governing body behind it. [Study Notes 3]

Front and Back of a Ten Dollar Banana Note

Front and Back of a One Dollar Banana Note

The *1st July1941, Ten-Cents-Note* issued by the Board of Commissioners of Currency of Malaya serves as a poignant example of the volatility of fiat currencies. During the period of Japanese occupation from 1942 to 1945, the Ten-Cents-Note with all the Notes issued by the Board of Commissioners of Currency of Malaya were outlawed and replaced by Japanese-issued *"Banana Notes"*. However, after Japan's surrender at the end of World War II and the British reoccupation of Singapore, the **Ten-Cents-Note** was once again recognised as legal tender, while the *"Banana Notes"* became worthless.

This scenario underscores one of the key characteristics of fiat currencies: ***their value is entirely dependent on the authority backing them***. In times of political upheaval, when a government or occupying force loses power or control, the value of the currency issued by that government can be wiped out, as was the case with *"Banana Notes"*.

For those who had saved their wealth in *"Banana Notes"* during the Japanese occupation, their savings evaporated overnight when the British returned. This harsh reality highlights the risks of holding onto fiat money in times of political or economic instability, where the value of currency can change drastically depending on the prevailing authority or government.

A Ten Cents Malaya Note issued by the Board of Commissioners of Currency of Malaya, dated 1st July 1941.

"SELF-IMMOLATION" OF A FIAT CURRENCY

The **Republic of Zimbabwe** emerged in April 1980 from the former Republic of Rhodesia. Initially, the country issued Zimbabwean dollars (Z$) in denominations of Z$2, Z$5, Z$10 and Z$20. However, in the 1990s, under President Robert Mugabe, Zimbabwe embarked on controversial land reforms, where land was seized from white farmers and redistributed to black farmers who were often ill-prepared and lacked the necessary skills to manage the farms. This resulted in a sharp decline in agricultural productivity, causing a severe drop in food production and an overall economic downturn.

As the economy deteriorated, Zimbabwe saw a dramatic rise in unemployment and political instability. The government's economic mismanagement, compounded by widespread corruption and political violence, led to a loss of confidence in both the Zimbabwe Dollar and the ruling government. As inflation spiralled, it eventually turned into hyperinflation. By 2003, the inflation rate had skyrocketed to nearly 600%, and by 2007, a loaf of bread could cost up to *10 billion Zimbabwe Dollars*, with prices doubling daily in some cases.

In response, the Zimbabwean government began issuing larger and larger denominations of banknotes, but this only added to the sense of instability. As the Zimbabwe Dollar lost its purchasing power, citizens increasingly turned to foreign currencies, with the USD becoming the primary medium of exchange for everyday transactions.

In April 2024, Zimbabwe introduced a new currency, the **ZIG**, which is backed by gold to stabilise the economy and restore confidence in its monetary system. This marked an end to the era of hyperinflation and the need to continually add extra zeros to Zimbabwe's currency. The ZIG aims to bring a sense of stability and trust back to the nation's financial system, providing hope for a more sustainable and reliable currency future.

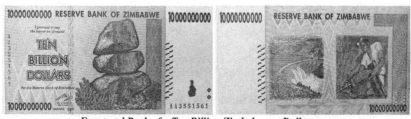

Front and Back of a Ten Billion Zimbabwean Dollar

QUIRKY FIAT CURRENCY

The Union Bank of Burma established in 1948 was given the exclusive right to issue banknotes in Burma. The "Rupee" was subsequently changed to "Kyat". The "15", "35" and "75" Kyat notes all depicted the Burma war hero General Aung Sun. These notes were launched between 1985 to 1986 and were *demonetised* (*no longer acceptable*) when the new Military Junta took power, with **Burma** renamed **Myanmar** in 1989 and its capital **"Rangoon"** changed to **"Yangon"**. The denominations of the three notes are unique in that each of them ends with "five" instead of the usual "zero", which is a rarity of its own kind.

OVERCOMING U.S. DOLLAR ADDICTION

When the Bretton Woods System was established, the United States held significant dominance in global trade, making the USD the preferred reserve currency, underpinned by the Gold Standard. However, as the European Economic Community (EEC) and Japan experienced rapid economic growth post-Bretton Woods, the U.S.'s dominance in international trade began to wane. This, coupled with persistent U.S. balance of payments deficits, eroded confidence in the USD as the world's reserve currency.

Despite this, the U.S. maintained its hegemony largely due to its influence over global markets, particularly in the energy sector. The U.S. and Saudi Arabia's agreement to trade oil in USD (creating the "petrodollar") established the USD as the primary currency for global commodity trading. This practice was soon adopted for other commodities, ensuring the USD's central role in international transactions.

The reliance on USD for pricing commodities made it hard to break this dependency, as the loss of the USD's reserve currency status could lead to market dislocations and poorer price transparency. The U.S. also maintained its dominance through its leadership in international institutions like the IMF and the World Bank, which were integral to global trade and finance. The size of the U.S. economy, combined with its consumer power, meant that many countries were still compelled to use the USD in trade, even as the U.S.'s relative economic power declined post-Bretton Woods.

However, this status is now being challenged, particularly by China's RMB. Since China began liberalising its economy in 1979, its rapid growth has put it on a trajectory to close the gap with the U.S. economy, raising the possibility of the RMB becoming a more significant player in global trade and finance. The challenge to the USD's reserve currency status is now a key issue in international economics.

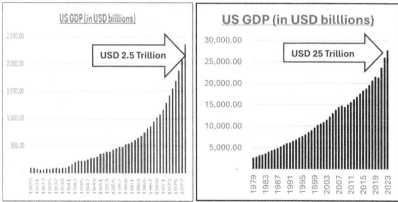

Figure 2b: *U.S. GDP from 1929 to 1978*   **Figure 2c:** *U.S. GDP from 1979 to 2023*
U.S. GDP Data, U.S. Bureau of Economic Analysis

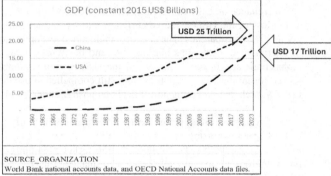

Figure 2d: *U.S. and China GDP from 1930 to 2023*

Gross Domestic Product (GDP) is the total monetary value of all goods and services produced within a country over a specific period, typically measured annually. It essentially represents the "income" a country earns from producing and selling goods and services. A growing GDP often signals a healthy economy, as it generally reflects higher business production and increased consumer spending.

This was evident with China's economic rise beginning in the 1980s when the country opened its economy. China became known as the ***"Factory of the World",*** as it rapidly expanded its manufacturing base and became a global hub for producing goods. This led to significant exports, particularly to major trading partners like the United States. During periods of rapid growth, China's exports often outpaced imports by a large margin, contributing substantially to its GDP growth. This economic boom continued through the Global Financial Crisis (GFC) period, further cementing China's place as a major global economic player.

Chapter 3
Collusion, Collaboration, Clashes and Disputes
The negatives of trade collusions and the positives of collaborations. The issues of currency manipulations, interventions and pegs. Disputes brewing between China and U.S.

International trade has long depended heavily on the U.S. Dollar (USD), serving as a common "language" for global transactions. The USD's role is pivotal due to its functions in price discovery, clearing systems and its adoption by market participants for trade. This twin functionality of the USD for both collaboration and collusion is akin to the duality of Dr. Jekyll and Mr. Hyde. While collaboration aligns with the original goals of the Bretton Woods Agreement, the volatility of the USD, driven by trade imbalances, investment flows and market speculation, has revealed its more unpredictable side.

The abandonment of the Bretton Woods System led to exponential growth in cross-border trade and investment flows, with USD dominating as the transactional currency. This period saw a proliferation of trading counterparties and financial players, creating immense flows of USD across jurisdictions and solidifying its role in the global economy.

In fiction, the concept of collusion is vividly depicted in the 1971 James Bond movie ***Diamonds are Forever***. The villains hoard diamonds, manipulating their value and use them to build a satellite laser weapon, threatening world leaders. In a dramatic climax, Bond dismantles their operation, destroys the weapon and thwarts the mastermind Blofeld's scheme. While such cinematic villainy may seem far-fetched, collusion and manipulation are very real in global trade and finance, albeit without the theatrics of secret bases and laser-equipped satellites. The USD, much like the diamonds in the movie, can be a tool for both order and exploitation in the intricate web of international commerce.

COLLUSION IN INTERNATIONAL TRADE

Collusion in international trade refers to secret agreements between businesses, governments or trade organisations aimed at manipulating markets for mutual benefit. These practices undermine fair competition and often harm consumers, taxpayers and smaller players in the market.

One form of collusion is ***price-fixing***, where businesses agree to set prices at predetermined levels instead of letting market forces decide. This results in artificially high prices, reducing affordability and placing a burden on consumers. Another common practice is ***bid-rigging***, where companies manipulate the outcomes of competitive bidding processes for government contracts or large projects, leading to inflated costs and misallocation of resources.

Market allocation is another tactic, where firms or countries divide markets geographically or by product type to ensure exclusive control. This limits competition, reduces consumer choice and often leads to higher prices. Similarly, ***exclusive agreements*** between companies and suppliers or distributors restrict competitors' access to essential distribution channels, consolidating market dominance and stifling competitive pricing.

Countries may also engage in ***coordinated tariffs***, imposing harmonised trade barriers to protect local industries. While this can shield domestic producers, it often raises consumer costs and reduces the variety and quality of available products.

These collusive practices distort the principles of free trade, suppress innovation and burden consumers. To preserve fair competition and market efficiency, robust international regulations and enforcement mechanisms are essential.

OPEC, the Organisation of Petroleum Exporting Countries, has long acted as a cartel, coordinating oil production among its members to manipulate global prices. While this collusion would be illegal under many national competition laws, it is permitted under international law due to the sovereignty of its member states.

OPEC's control over oil supply has had widespread economic impacts, including price volatility, inflation and increasing production costs of factory inputs for oil-importing nations. In response, many countries have sought alternatives like wind, solar and nuclear energy to reduce reliance on oil and enhance energy security. While OPEC's actions benefit its members, they have also accelerated the global shift toward more sustainable energy solutions. [1]

In 2013, nine Japanese auto-parts manufacturers were fined a total of $740 million by the U.S. Department of Justice (DOJ) for operating an illegal price-fixing cartel. Over a decade (2000-2010), the cartel's executives and co-conspirators used covert meetings and coded language to rig bids, fix prices and allocate the supply of auto parts to U.S. car manufacturers. These practices inflated costs for automakers, ultimately penalising consumers.

The cartel's activities, conducted primarily in USD, left a financial trail that passed through the U.S. clearing system, thereby aiding its eventual detection. The DOJ's investigation involved collaboration with global regulators, including the Japanese Fair-Trade Commission, European Commission, and others from Canada, Korea, Mexico and Australia, demonstrating the international effort required to expose and dismantle such schemes. [2]

Up until 1999, Microsoft was widely recognised as a monopoly due to its dominance in the Windows Operating System (OS) market. The company bundled its Internet Explorer (IE) browser with Windows OS and offered its suite of products, such as Microsoft Office, through exclusionary contracts with PC manufacturers and Internet Service Providers (ISPs). These contracts discouraged manufacturers and ISPs from offering competing browsers or software, limiting consumer choice. Additionally, Microsoft's aggressive pricing strategies stifled innovation and blocked potential competitors from entering the market.

The U.S. Department of Justice (DOJ) and several state attorneys general filed a legal case against Microsoft, accusing it of leveraging its OS monopoly to suppress competition, deprive consumers of choice and hinder innovation. The case aimed to break up the company, but this was ultimately avoided when Microsoft agreed to ***behavioural remedies***. These included sharing technical information with competitors to enable the development of Windows-compatible software and allowing PC manufacturers to install other web browsers on Windows-based systems.

This landmark case paved the way for new entrants like Google Chrome and Mozilla Firefox to compete in the browser market. It also fostered a more competitive environment, enabling companies like Google, Apple and Amazon to grow, shaping the modern technology landscape to the benefit of consumers. [3], [4]

The rising demand for electric vehicles (EVs), driven by the need to reduce urban emissions, has seen China's EV manufacturers gain significant market share in the U.S. and Europe. Between 2020 and 2023, Chinese EV exports to the US and EU surged, raising concerns for President Joe Biden and the European Union (EU) on the potential threat to domestic automakers and the risk of widespread job losses.

In response, the U.S. Congress imposed a 100% tariff on Chinese EV imports, while the EU enacted an additional 35% tariff in October 2024. These coordinated tariffs aim to curb Chinese EV exports to protect domestic industries. Enforcement measures could include U.S. government orders for clearing banks to halt USD settlements for Chinese EV-related transactions.

As the EU's additional tariff deadline approached in October 2024, China and the EU agreed to hold further negotiations, exploring alternatives to tariffs on China-built EVs, signalling the potential for a diplomatic resolution to the trade tensions. [5]

Orange juice, a popular breakfast staple, is often subject to price fluctuations due to weather conditions that affect orange yields. To manage this risk, orange futures see [Box 3A] contracts are traded on commodity exchanges, allowing farmers and traders to hedge against price volatility.

In 1989, a major market manipulation scheme came to light involving Louis Dreyfuss, Citrus Associates of the Americas and trader Anthony DeAngelis. The group was accused by the Commodity Futures Trading Commission (CFTC) of manipulating the orange juice market by stockpiling large quantities of frozen orange juice. [6] Their goal was to create a false sense of scarcity, driving up prices and enabling them to profit from the inflated market.

This manipulation scheme mirrored the tactics of the fictional villain Blofeld in James Bond's Diamonds Are Forever, where the buildup of inventory (in this case, diamonds) was used to control prices. While diamonds may last forever, the same can't be said for orange juice, which eventually spoils and loses value, highlighting the temporary nature of such manipulations in agricultural markets.

[Box 3A]
Derivatives, Futures, Leverage, Margin Calls, and Borrowing Explained:
Derivatives *are financial contracts whose value is derived from an underlying asset, such as stocks, commodities or currencies.* **Futures**, *a type of derivative, are agreements to buy or sell an asset at a predetermined price on a future date. These contracts are often traded with* **leverage**, *which allows investors to control a large position with a small upfront investment. Leverage amplifies potential gains but also increases risks, as losses can exceed the initial amount invested. To trade futures, investors must maintain a margin account, a deposit with the broker to cover potential losses. If the account's value falls below a required threshold due to adverse price movements, a* **margin call** *is issued, requiring the investor to add funds to avoid liquidation.* **Borrowing**, *common in leveraged trading, further amplifies risks, as traders must repay loans regardless of whether their investments yield profits or losses.*

COLLUSION CONSEQUENCES

Collusion in markets harms consumers by reducing competition, which leads to higher prices and fewer choices. Companies that engage in anti-competitive practices are less motivated to innovate or improve efficiency, focusing instead on maintaining their market dominance. This results in market distortion, where colluding firms can achieve short-term profits at the cost of long-term economic inefficiencies.

Larger, established companies often benefit more from collusion, creating barriers that prevent smaller or newer firms from entering the market. This can exacerbate economic inequality across businesses and countries. To prevent such practices, national and global organisations, like the World Trade Organisation (WTO) or regional bodies like the European Commission, monitor trade and enforce fair competition. These institutions can impose penalties such as hefty fines, trade restrictions or other sanctions on companies or countries found guilty of collusion, ensuring that there are legal repercussions for such activities.

To prevent collusion, governments and international bodies must work together through competition laws, antitrust regulations and trade agreements. Promoting transparency and encouraging healthy competition are key strategies to deter anti-competitive behaviours. Penalties for collusion, such as fines or trade restrictions, help to ensure that offenders are held accountable.

Since many collusive practices cross borders, global cooperation between regulators and policymakers is essential. This cooperation ensures that colluding parties cannot evade penalties by exploiting jurisdictional boundaries. By working together, nations can maintain the integrity of global trade and create a fairer, more competitive environment for businesses and consumers alike.

COLLABORATION IN ACTION

International trade collaboration is the process through which countries work together to promote economic growth, development and peace. This collaboration takes place at various levels, from bilateral agreements between two countries to multilateral and regional agreements involving multiple nations. These partnerships are essential for fostering economic interdependence, which can lead to shared prosperity and peaceful resolution of conflicts.

Bilateral agreements involve two countries negotiating specific trade terms, such as reducing tariffs or opening up markets to each other. Examples include the U.S.-Japan Trade Agreement and the Canada-South Korea Free Trade Agreement, where the focus is on fostering deeper economic ties between the two nations.

On a larger scale, ***multilateral agreements*** are more complex because they involve multiple countries. The World Trade Organisation (WTO) plays a central role in these agreements by creating binding trade rules designed to ensure fairness and a level playing field in global commerce. These agreements aim to reduce trade barriers across many countries, enabling more fluid and fair-trade practices worldwide.

Regional trade agreements are generally easier to negotiate due to fewer participants. These agreements often involve countries within a specific geographical area and are designed to reduce trade barriers within the region. The European Union (EU), the United States-Mexico-Canada Agreement (USMCA) and Mercosur in South America are prime examples of regional trade agreements that enhance cooperation among neighbouring countries, making it easier for them to trade goods and services with one another.

Several key elements underpin successful international trade collaboration. ***Trade facilitation*** focuses on streamlining processes and improving infrastructure to ensure goods move efficiently across borders. For example, the WTO's Trade Facilitation Agreement aims to simplify customs procedures, which reduces delays and costs. ***Regulatory harmonisation*** is another crucial element, where countries align their regulations to reduce trade barriers. This makes it easier for goods to be traded without facing excessive regulatory hurdles. In addition, effective ***dispute resolution*** mechanisms, such as the WTO's Dispute Settlement Mechanism, allow countries to resolve trade conflicts in a fair and structured manner, which helps maintain stability in the global trade system. Lastly, ***technical cooperation and capacity building*** allow developed countries or international organisations to assist developing nations in improving their trade infrastructure and capabilities, making them more competitive in the global market.

International trade organisations like the WTO, the International Monetary Fund (IMF), the World Bank and the United Nations Conference on Trade and Development (UNCTAD) play vital roles in supporting these collaborations. The WTO oversees trade rules and helps resolve disputes, the IMF provides financial stability and support to countries facing economic crises, the World Bank funds infrastructure projects to enhance trade and UNCTAD focuses on integrating developing countries into the global economy.

Together, these efforts help to reduce barriers, resolve conflicts and foster economic growth, creating a more interconnected, peaceful and prosperous world.

COLLABORATION BENEFITS

International trade collaboration brings a host of benefits that contribute to global economic growth and stability. One of the key advantages is ***access to new markets***. By partnering with other countries, nations can expand their reach and increase exports, opening new opportunities for businesses. This growth in exports can help stimulate domestic industries and boost overall economic performance.

Economic growth is another significant benefit of trade collaboration. When countries collaborate on trade, they can increase their export potential, which enhances the efficiency of their industries. This often leads to the creation of new jobs, stimulating employment and improving living standards. Additionally, exposure to international competition encourages innovation. As companies face global rivals, they are pushed to improve their products and services, adopting new technologies and best practices that drive productivity and creativity.

For consumers, trade collaboration brings immediate benefits. Trade agreements often reduce tariffs and eliminate other barriers, leading to lower prices for goods and services. Consumers gain access to a wider variety of products, often with better quality and safety standards, which improves overall consumer protection and satisfaction.

Furthermore, international trade fosters peace. The ***economic interdependence*** that results from trade collaboration creates incentives for nations to resolve conflicts peacefully. Countries with strong trade ties are more likely to cooperate on global issues, such as climate change, health pandemics and security.

Finally, international trade can be particularly beneficial for developing countries. It gives them *improved access* to global markets, which can result in higher incomes, better job opportunities and poverty reduction. Organisations like the WTO and the World Bank work to make trade more inclusive, ensuring that all countries, regardless of their development status, can share in the benefits.

International trade collaboration not only drives economic growth but also encourages innovation, fosters peace and supports sustainable development. Its benefits extend to both developed and developing nations, contributing to a more interconnected and prosperous global economy.

COLLABORATION CHALLENGES

Despite the many benefits of international trade collaboration, several challenges continue to create friction between nations. These obstacles often complicate the process of maintaining open and cooperative trade relations.

One of the most significant challenges is *protectionist policies*, such as high tariffs, subsidies for domestic industries and import quotas. While these measures are designed to protect local industries from foreign competition, they can often lead to trade disputes, retaliatory actions and a breakdown in cooperation between countries. Protectionist policies can distort markets, drive up consumer prices and ultimately hinder the global economic growth that trade collaboration aims to foster.

Another issue is *unequal benefits* from international trade. Developed nations, with their advanced industries, infrastructure and technological advantages, typically benefit more from trade, while developing countries may struggle to compete on an equal footing. This disparity in trade benefits can create tensions and make collaboration efforts fragile and unsustainable. Developing nations may feel left behind or disadvantaged, which could weaken their commitment to global trade cooperation in the long term.

Further complicating matters are *disagreements over trade rules*. Issues such as intellectual property rights, labour standards and environmental regulations often lead to disputes between countries. These disagreements can take years to resolve, requiring extensive negotiation and a delicate balancing of interests. If trade rules are unclear or inconsistent, they can delay or even derail trade agreements, which makes international collaboration more difficult and uncertain.

Additionally, *economic nationalism and domestic pressures* also pose significant barriers. As countries increasingly prioritise domestic industries and jobs, political pressures can drive governments to impose trade barriers such as tariffs or quotas. This protectionist stance can slow the momentum of global trade cooperation, reducing the potential for mutually beneficial agreements.

Despite these challenges, international trade collaboration remains a critical driver of global economic growth, job creation and international peace. For trade collaboration to continue thriving, strong governance is essential. Transparent, well-enforced agreements and sustained cooperation are necessary to ensure the benefits of trade are shared equitably, and that disputes are resolved efficiently.

While protectionism and unequal trade benefits present obstacles, the trend toward globalisation and interconnectedness encourages nations to seek greater collaboration.

Countries that resist cooperation or adopt protectionist policies risk isolating themselves, which could hinder their long-term economic success. In a globally connected economy, nations that fail to collaborate may ultimately struggle to remain competitive and prosperous.

CURRENCY MANIPULATION

During the Bretton Woods era, the global community worked to prevent currency devaluation from becoming a widespread tool for enhancing export competitiveness. The idea behind this was that a weaker currency could make a country's goods cheaper, thus boosting exports. However, such *"beggar thy neighbour"* strategies were discouraged, as they could spark retaliatory devaluations among trading nations, leading to a destabilising effect on the global monetary system. The fear was that a series of countries devaluing their currencies in response to other countries' devaluations would undermine stability and disrupt international trade.

China's approach to managing its currency, renminbi (RMB), has been a subject of considerable international debate. For years, China pegged its currency to the USD, which allowed it to maintain an artificially low exchange rate. This made Chinese exports cheaper and more competitive globally, enabling China to build large trade surpluses with countries like the United States. As a result, China accumulated massive foreign currency reserves, primarily in USD. This fuelled accusations that it was manipulating its currency for economic gain.

The United States expressed frustration with China's currency policies, accusing the country of unfairly manipulating its currency to gain trade advantages *(like pegging below the actual market exchange rate value)*. In 2019, the U.S. Treasury officially labelled China a currency manipulator, although this designation was lifted in early 2020 after trade negotiations made some progress. Politicians and critics argued that China's undervalued currency had contributed to the decline of U.S. manufacturing and the loss of jobs, as it allowed Chinese goods to flood the market at prices lower than those of American-made products.

However, China defended its currency management as essential for maintaining economic stability. Chinese authorities explained that controlling the RMB's value helped manage inflation, reduce economic volatility and protect its developing economy from external financial shocks. This strategy proved to be particularly effective during the Asian Financial Crisis of 1997. While many neighbouring countries, such as Thailand, Malaysia and Indonesia, saw their currencies devalue sharply during the crisis, China's currency remained stable, with the RMB/USD exchange rate fixed between 8.25 and 8.32. This stability helped China avoid the financial turmoil that affected other Asian economies. (Figure 3a)

In summary, China's currency management strategy, particularly its decision to peg the RMB to the USD, has been a key element in shaping its trade relationships and international economic standing.

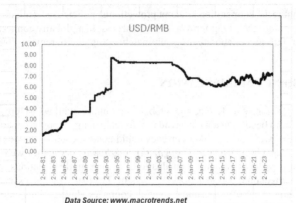

Figure 3a: *USD/RMB Exchange Rates maintained between 8.25 and 8.32 during the financial crisis in 1997.*

In recent years, Chinese authorities have emphasised a gradual appreciation of the RMB through a series of reforms aimed at liberalising the currency. China has moved toward a more market-driven exchange rate system, though it remains heavily managed within an unofficial trading band. This band is maintained through currency interventions by the People's Bank of China (PBOC). The International Monetary Fund (IMF) has provided positive affirmations of China's currency policies, concluding that the RMB is no longer significantly undervalued, although questions regarding full market determination persist. The RMB-USD peg has transitioned into a managed float system within an established trading band.

Despite these efforts toward reform, currency manipulation accusations have often surfaced during times of trade tension, particularly between China and the United States. The trade war between these two economic superpowers, which began in 2018, saw tariffs imposed on billions of USD worth of goods, with China's currency policies being a central point of contention. This highlighted the need for international monetary cooperation.

China's currency management practices have sparked concerns at global institutions such as the WTO and the G20 (*an inter-governmental forum of 19 countries, European Union and African Union*). Some countries have called for stricter international rules to prevent currency manipulation, viewing it as a form of trade protectionism. However, enforcing such rules remains challenging due to the lack of clear policies or universally accepted guidelines among WTO members.

The lessons from the Bretton Woods system suggest that establishing a universal set of rules for currency exchange is nearly impossible. Instead, a more effective approach may involve fostering bilateral or multilateral symbiotic trading relationships, which naturally balance trade flows. This approach will help minimise trade imbalances and, over time, contribute to the stability of currency exchange rates, reducing the risk of manipulation and promoting more sustainable international trade relations.

The *frayed tempers* that once led other countries to accuse China of currency manipulation have faded, but the issue continues to linger in the background of broader economic and trade disputes. In recent years, China's currency, the RMB, has appreciated significantly, moving away from its previously rigid control. The Chinese government has also taken steps to internationalise the RMB, including successfully pushing for its inclusion in the IMF's Special Drawing Rights (SDR) basket of reserve currencies, a major milestone in enhancing its global influence. *(Special Drawing Rights (SDRs) is an international reserve asset created by the IMF to supplement countries' official reserves. Their value is based on a basket of major currencies (USD, EUR, RMB, JPY, GBP), and they can be exchanged between countries to provide liquidity in times of financial need.)*

Despite these advancements, concerns persist about the possibility of China resuming currency manipulation, especially if it faces economic pressures. These concerns are amplified by China's slowing growth, ongoing debt restructurings in its real estate markets and the global uncertainties stemming from trade conflicts and the spillover effects of the COVID-19 pandemic. While China has been officially labelled a currency manipulator in the past, the debate over whether the country still engages in such practices remains unresolved.

As China's economic and geopolitical influence continues to grow, its currency policies are increasingly scrutinised by international policymakers and governments. The issue is particularly sensitive given the economic competition between China and other major economies, most notably the United States, as well as the broader geopolitical tensions that impact trade and finance. In this context, the management of China's currency will continue to be a key area of focus, balancing economic stability with global expectations for fair trade practices.

CURRENCY INTERVENTION

Currency interventions are deliberate actions taken by a country's central bank or government to influence the value of its national currency in the foreign exchange market. The primary goal of such interventions is to stabilise or alter the currency's value relative to other currencies, with the aim of achieving various economic objectives like controlling inflation, promoting exports and responding to economic crises.

One of the primary reasons for currency interventions is to ***promote exports***. By weakening the national currency, a country can make its goods and services cheaper and more competitive in international markets. For example, China has historically intervened in the currency markets to keep the RMB undervalued, making Chinese exports more attractive to markets such as the U.S. and Europe, thus boosting the country's export sector and improving its trade balance.

Another key motivation for currency interventions is to ***control inflation***. A central bank may intervene in the foreign exchange markets to strengthen its currency if inflation begins rising too quickly. A stronger currency makes imports cheaper, which can help reduce domestic inflation by lowering the cost of imported goods and raw materials. For instance, in the early 2000s, Brazil's central bank sold foreign currency reserves and raised interest rates to support the Brazilian Real (BRL), aiming to counteract high inflation and stabilise the economy.

Stabilising currency fluctuations is also a common goal for central banks. Rapid appreciation or depreciation of a national currency can destabilise an economy, so countries often intervene to prevent such fluctuations. Japan, for instance, has repeatedly intervened to stabilise the yen (JPY) during periods of economic uncertainty, especially when the JPY's rapid appreciation threatened to harm Japan's export-driven economy.

Currency interventions can also be a response to capital flight, where investors move their money out of the country, putting pressure on the national currency. In such cases, central banks may act to prevent a sharp depreciation by buying their own currency in exchange for foreign currencies. Argentina, for example, has faced numerous economic crises, during which the central bank intervened to support the Argentinian Peso (ARS) and prevent rapid depreciation, thus maintaining some level of economic stability.

Some countries opt for *exchange rate pegs* to another currency, often the U.S. dollar (USD) or the Euro (EUR), to maintain stability. These countries must intervene in the foreign exchange markets to defend the peg by buying or selling their own currency when it deviates from the target rate.

Hong Kong is a well-known example, where the Hong Kong dollar (HKD) is pegged to the USD. The Hong Kong Monetary Authority (HKMA) regularly intervenes in the currency markets to ensure the peg is maintained.

Countries with significant trade imbalances may also intervene in currency markets to adjust their currency value, aiming to improve their balance of payments. A devalued currency can make imports more expensive and exports cheaper, thereby improving the trade balance. For instance, India has occasionally intervened to manage the value of the Indian rupee (INR), particularly when capital outflows put downward pressure on the currency. The Reserve Bank of India (RBI) has responded by selling USD to buy INR, attempting to support the currency.

Finally, currency interventions can be part of a broader economic strategy to stimulate growth. When a country's currency becomes too strong, it can make exports expensive and harm the domestic economy. In the early 2010s, Switzerland intervened to weaken the Swiss franc (CHF), which had been appreciating too rapidly. This appreciation made Swiss goods more expensive on international markets, hurting the export sector. By intervening in the currency market, Switzerland aimed to keep its economy competitive.

In sum, currency interventions are a powerful tool used by countries to manage economic stability, promote exports, control inflation and address various financial imbalances. However, these interventions can also raise concerns, particularly when countries are accused of manipulating their currency to gain trade advantages, leading to tensions in the global market.

CHINA (RMB Devaluation, 2015)

In August 2015, China's central bank, the People's Bank of China (PBOC), devalued the RMB by approximately 2% to counter slowing economic growth and declining exports. The move aimed to make Chinese exports more competitive, as a stronger RMB had been hurting their export growth amid weaker global demand. However, the devaluation caused global financial market turmoil, as investors feared it could trigger a *"Currency War"* with other countries potentially devaluing their currencies in response. The move also intensified accusations of currency manipulation, particularly from the U.S., further escalating trade tensions.

JAPAN (JPY Intervention, Multiple Times)

Japan has long intervened in currency markets to prevent the JPY from appreciating too much, especially during times of global economic uncertainty. In the 1990s, the JPY was seen as a safe-haven currency, with investors buying it during crises, which drove up its value. To protect its export-driven economy, Japan's central bank, the Bank of Japan (BoJ), frequently intervened by selling JPY and purchasing USD to maintain competitiveness for Japanese exporters.

However, from 2023 to 2024, the situation reversed. The rapid rise in U.S. interest rates, aimed at controlling inflation, widened the interest rate gap between the U.S. and Japan, weakening the JPY. The JPY depreciated sharply from 120:1 against the USD to 160:1, increasing import costs (especially oil) and eroding Japan's trade surplus. Speculative bets on further JPY depreciation intensified the decline, prompting the BoJ to intervene by selling USD to buy JPY. However, this strategy was not sustainable, as the U.S.-Japan interest rate gap, driven by Japan's ultra-loose monetary policy, remained. In 2024, the BoJ eventually ended its zero-interest-rate policy (ZIRP) and raised rates twice to stabilise the USD/JPY exchange rate.

ARGENTINA (Peso Stabilisation, Multiple Times)

Argentina has often intervened in currency markets to stabilise the Argentine peso during economic crises, typically by selling foreign currency reserves to prevent rapid depreciation. These interventions aim to avoid hyperinflation, protect savings and curb capital flight during periods of financial instability. While such measures can offer short-term relief, they often deplete foreign reserves and fail to resolve the underlying economic issues, leading to prolonged volatility in the peso's value.

During times of *hyperinflation*, prices in Argentina can rise drastically. For example, a carton of milk could cost 10-20% more in the afternoon than it did in the morning, an extreme sign of hyperinflation, where currency value erodes quickly and unpredictably.

Argentina 100 Peso Note issued by Banco Central De La Republica Argentina

RUSSIA (Ruble Crisis, 2014-2015)

Following economic sanctions imposed due to the annexation of Crimea and a dramatic fall in oil prices, the Russian Ruble (RUB) came under severe pressure, losing about half of its value in late 2014. The Central Bank of Russia intervened to stabilise the RUB by raising interest rates to 17% and selling foreign currency reserves. The interventions initially slowed the RUB's decline but also caused economic contraction due to high interest rates. Eventually, Russia shifted toward a more flexible exchange rate policy and found alternative markets for her oil and natural gas.

Intervention Merits and Demerits

Currency interventions are powerful tools used by central banks to manage exchange rate volatility, promote economic goals and stabilise financial markets. While interventions can provide short-term benefits, there are often risks associated with it, such as depleting foreign reserves, creating market distortions or triggering retaliation from other countries. The decision to intervene must be carefully balanced with broader economic objectives and global market conditions.

CURRENCY PEGS

A currency peg fixes a country's exchange rate to a more stable currency, like the USD or EUR, to promote economic stability, reduce inflation and encourage trade. Hong Kong has pegged its currency to the USD since 1983 for stability and trade, while Cambodia uses a peg due to its dollarised economy and reliance on foreign investment. Both benefit from predictable exchange rates that foster confidence and trade.

HONG KONG DOLLAR PEG

Hong Kong has pegged its currency, the Hong Kong dollar (HKD), to the U.S. dollar (USD) at approximately HKD 7.80 per USD since 1983 through the Linked Exchange Rate System (LERS). [7] The Hong Kong Monetary Authority (HKMA) ensures the peg by intervening in the foreign exchange market when needed. This peg provides economic stability, reduces currency fluctuations and promotes trade and investment. It supports Hong Kong's role as a global financial hub by ensuring currency stability, encouraging capital flows and maintaining investor confidence. Pegging the HKD also helps keep inflation low, as the stable USD anchors inflation expectations, though it limits Hong Kong's monetary policy independence.

A Ten Hong Kong Dollar (HKD) note likely issued in the late 1960s. Chartered Bank and Standard Bank merged to become Standard Chartered Bank in 1969.

Pegging the Hong Kong dollar (HKD) to the U.S. dollar (USD) means the Hong Kong Monetary Authority (HKMA) loses monetary policy autonomy, effectively importing U.S. monetary policy. If U.S. interest rates rise or fall, Hong Kong must follow, even if local conditions suggest a different approach. This becomes particularly challenging when the U.S. Federal Reserve's policy diverges from Hong Kong's needs. During times of financial stress or geopolitical tension, the demand for USD often outstrips that for HKD, putting pressure on the peg. To defend it, the HKMA sells USD to buy HKD, depleting its foreign reserves. Despite occasional speculative attacks, the HKMA has managed to maintain the peg successfully.

CAMBODIAN KHMER RIEL PEG

Cambodia operates a dual currency system where the U.S. dollar (USD) is widely used alongside the Cambodian Khmer Riel (KHR). While the Riel is nominally the national currency, the USD dominates, accounting for about 80-90% of the money supply. This de facto dollarisation stems from Cambodia's post-civil war economic instability, where the introduction of the USD helped stabilise the economy following hyperinflation and the collapse of the Khmer Riel.

Using the USD has provided economic stability, facilitated trade and boosted foreign investment by reducing currency risk for businesses and investors. It has also helped control inflation, as the USD is more stable than the riel. However, Cambodia's reliance on the USD means it lacks control over its own monetary policy, with interest rates set by the U.S. Federal Reserve rather than the National Bank of Cambodia (NBC). The NBC also faces challenges in promoting the riel for domestic transactions, as the USD remains dominant in private dealings.

As Cambodia's economy grows, it may face challenges from its heavy reliance on the USD, including vulnerability to shifts in U.S. monetary policy, which could lead to higher borrowing costs or reduced investment. The future of Cambodia's currency peg, which loosely ties the riel to the USD at around KHR 4000 to USD 1, will depend on how well the country can balance its dollarised economy with the promotion of its own currency.

A Hundred Cambodian Khmer Riel (KHR) note issued by the National Bank of Cambodia.

A Hundred Cambodian Khmer Riel (KHR) old note issued by the Banque Nationale du Cambodge, pre-Khmer Rouge period.

To Peg or not to Peg

Both Hong Kong and Cambodia maintain currency systems, Hong Kong through a formal peg to the USD and Cambodia through a more informal dollarised economy, to ensure economic stability, promote trade and control inflation. Hong Kong's peg is carefully managed by the HKMA to maintain exchange rate stability and foster confidence in its financial system. Cambodia, on the other hand, relies heavily on the USD in everyday transactions, with the Cambodian riel (KHR) playing a minimal role in the economy.

However, both systems come with trade-offs, primarily the loss of monetary policy independence. Since both economies are tethered to the USD, their interest rates and monetary conditions are largely dictated by U.S. economic policies. This means that Hong Kong must align its interest rates with those set by the U.S. Federal Reserve, even when domestic economic conditions may warrant a different approach. Similarly, Cambodia's reliance on the USD limits the ability of the National Bank of Cambodia to implement independent monetary policies as it does not control the supply of USD in the country.

Despite these limitations, both systems have provided stability, fostered trade and attracted foreign investment, which have been crucial for their economic growth. However, as these economies evolve, their dependence on the USD may present challenges, especially during periods of economic policy divergence from the U.S.

CLASHES: WEAPONISING THE USD

The USD has a dual role in global trade, functioning both as a tool for constructive trade facilitation and as a weapon for imposing economic sanctions.

In global trade, the USD is commonly used for transactions, providing ease of trade between nations even if they don't share the same currency. However, the U.S. government can leverage its control over the USD to impose sanctions or embargoes on non-compliant nations, limiting their access to international financial systems, such as USD clearing banks or the SWIFT system. For example, during World War II, the U.S. imposed trade sanctions on Japan, crippling its economy. More recently, trade sanctions imposed on Russia by the EU [8] in response to the Ukraine [9] invasion, or on Iran [10] for uranium production and missile development, illustrate how the USD can be applied to exert pressure on countries, often leading to severe economic consequences for both the targeted countries and their populations.

Trade sanctions and embargoes, such as those on Russia or Venezuela [11], aim to punish nations for political actions, hoping to force compliance. The U.S. has used sanctions to freeze assets, block international trade or disrupt economies, as seen in the 2019 sanctions on Venezuela's oil industry. While these sanctions can hurt a country's economy, they often harm the civilian population more than the intended political leaders, who may not face immediate consequences. Additionally, the imposition of sanctions can backfire, encouraging targeted nations to seek alternatives to the USD, which erodes the USD's dominance in global trade and finance.

There are consequences for weaponising the USD. The long-term effect of using the USD as a weapon is that it can prompt countries to seek alternatives, diminishing the USD's role as the world's primary reserve currency. While sanctions can be effective in some cases, such as during World War II or against apartheid-era South Africa, they often fail to achieve desired outcomes, causing collateral damage to global markets and economies. As a result, nations may increasingly look for alternative ways to conduct trade, creating new trading blocs and accelerating the search for a new global reserve currency. This dynamic could weaken the influence of the USD, undermining its credibility as a global financial anchor.

USD AS A UTILITY

A significant milestone in 2001 was China's accession to the World Trade Organisation (WTO).

Free Trade Agreements (FTAs) became more widespread, facilitating smoother trade by setting pre-defined procedures, protecting intellectual property and providing legal recourse for disputes. These agreements contributed to a faster and more efficient global trade environment, with the USD serving as the primary medium for exchange, pricing and clearing of transactions. The widespread use of the USD, supported by systems like SWIFT, helped maintain the flow of trade and financial transactions globally.

The **World Trade Organisation (WTO)**, which officially launched on January 1, 1995, marked a milestone for international trade, creating a platform for countries to agree on trade rules and norms. The inclusion of China in the WTO brought her into alignment with globally accepted trading practices. The WTO contributed to several achievements, including improving transparency, strengthening dispute settlement mechanisms and reducing barriers to trade, all of which reinforced the USD's role as the dominant currency for international trade. [12]

Most commodities, priced in USD, solidified the USD's position as the global reserve currency, enabling the smooth functioning of international trade and reinforcing the USD's role in global finance.

TRADE DISPUTES

After normalising diplomatic relations with the United States in 1979, China opened its economy, attracting substantial foreign investment that energised its manufacturing sector. Its export-led growth strategy enabled rapid economic expansion until 2007, with a slight slowdown after the Global Financial Crisis (GFC) in 2008. However, U.S.-China relations took a sharp negative turn with rising tensions. Following initial diplomatic exchanges between Xi Jinping and Joe Biden in January 2021, the U.S. imposed sanctions on certain Chinese firms over alleged human rights violations in Xinjiang, marking a period of intensified economic rivalry.

From 2021 to 2023, U.S.-China trade tensions escalated. The U.S. restricted China's access to key industries through export controls, tariffs and outright bans. Particularly in *semiconductors and advanced technologies*, the U.S. imposed controls on chips, artificial intelligence (AI) and supercomputing technologies, aiming to limit China's technological capabilities. Chinese firms like Huawei and ZTE faced U.S. operating bans over national security concerns, while disputes in *defence, aerospace* and *solar panel manufacturing* also emerged. The U.S. justified these actions as necessary for national security, while China countered by accusing the U.S. of exaggerating threats and adopting discriminatory trade practices. [13]

China argued that these restrictions harmed bilateral trade and economic cooperation, negatively impacting businesses in both nations. Critics warned that U.S. companies might lose Chinese market opportunities to competitors from other countries, eroding their global competitiveness. Moreover, these restrictions created ripple effects across international supply chains, increasing trade complexities for third-party nations linked to the restricted industries.

The ambiguous nature of these disputes, particularly in technology, makes arbitration under WTO regulations challenging. Prolonged disputes could result in minimal or at best, slow resolutions or require compromises, given the inherent complexity of such international trade conflicts.

This growing economic rivalry has prompted concerns among nations about the **"weaponisation" of the USD**. By leveraging the USD's dominance for sanctions and trade restrictions, the U.S. risks undermining the USD's credibility as a neutral reserve currency. Over time, such actions could erode global confidence in the USD, potentially chipping away at its reserve currency status.

Chapter 4
Economic Evolution and Crisis Management
A walk through the U.S. economic evolution, crisis management, tackling the twin deficits, the Federal Reserve's hand in influencing monetary policy and the Fed's rescue of the U.S. economy.

The vital foundations established within and beyond the borders of the United States over the years have given it the economic might it enjoys today. The U.S. has consistently demonstrated its ability to manage crises, both domestic and international, reinforcing its position as a global powerhouse. Its economic evolution has propelled the U.S. dollar (USD) to prominence on the world stage, empowering the nation to exert significant economic influence globally.

Winston Churchill once advised that we should *"look farther backward so that the farther forward we can see"*. This chapter adopts his perspective, albeit with a focus extending only as far back as the late 19th century. By examining the United States' journey from that period onward, an insightful perspective emerges on how the country evolved to its current economic stature. This historical reflection also provides a basis for speculating on where the nation and its currency might head in the future.

ECONOMIC EVOLUTION

From late 19th century, a period often known as the second industrial revolution, the United States experienced tremendous growth, notably in manufacturing. The sectors that benefitted were mainly steel, railroads, oil and finance. Fuelling this growth was the influx of immigrants from Europe by the millions. With rapid urbanisation, cities were born. Some served as manufacturing hubs whilst others became financial and trading centres.

Learning from Mistakes

The laissez-faire economic landscape of the 19th century saw the rise of powerful corporations like Standard Oil and U.S. Steel. These industrial goliaths exerted significant control over their respective sectors, prompting the government to introduce antitrust laws and regulations to curb monopolistic practices. This marked the beginning of a more structured approach to balancing corporate power with public interest.

At the same time, labour disputes began to surface. The rapid pace of industrialisation, driven by relentless corporate pursuit of profit, placed immense pressure on workers, often subjecting them to harsh working conditions and unfavourable employment terms. Inevitably, labour unrest grew, with strikes becoming a frequent occurrence. This period marked the early struggles between workers and capitalists, eventually leading to the rise of organised labour unions advocating for better rights and protections.

The emergence of economic cycles also became a notable feature of the era. The surge in investments during periods of growth fuelled a *"herd mentality"* among businesses. Overinvestment and overcrowded markets often led to a *"boom and bust"* phenomena, known today as economic or business cycles. A prime example of this was the Panic of 1893, a severe economic depression triggered by railroad bankruptcies and banking failures. This crisis resulted in widespread unemployment and political unrest, offering a stark lesson in the vulnerabilities of an unregulated market. [1]

*The sight of wildebeests, zebras and antelopes stampeding across the Serengeti Plains is a vivid illustration of **herd mentality** in nature. This instinctive behaviour, also known as **groupthink or mob behaviour**, demonstrates how individuals within a group often follow the actions and decisions of the majority, frequently disregarding their own instincts or assessments.*

*In humans, **herd mentality** drives individuals to conform their decisions, opinions or actions to those of the majority, often influenced by social pressures or the perceived wisdom of the crowd. This phenomenon is particularly evident in financial markets, where investors often rush to buy or sell based on popular sentiment, and this is also seen in social trends, where people adopt widely accepted views or behaviours without critical evaluation.*

***Herd mentality** can yield both positive and negative outcomes. For animals like wildebeests, zebras and antelopes, moving as a herd provides protection from predators and enables coordinated migration. However, it can also lead them into dangerous situations, such as stampedes or exposure to predators at crowded crossing points. Similarly, in humans, herd mentality can foster unity and collective action but can also drive irrational decision-making. When individuals blindly follow the crowd, disregarding their own perspectives, they risk succumbing to errors in judgment. This dynamic is often at play in the "boom and bust" cycles of economic systems, where mass behaviour inflates bubbles that inevitably burst, leading to widespread consequences.*

Ultimately, while herd mentality can bring order and collective strength, its pitfalls serve as a caution, reminding us of the importance of balancing group dynamics with individual critical thinking.

Progressive Reforms

The economic missteps of the past prompted a wave of progressive reforms aimed at curbing business excesses, improving labour conditions and enhancing consumer protection. In the early 20th century, numerous regulations and laws were enacted to promote fair practices and establish a transparent legal framework for trade and commerce. These measures laid the groundwork for a more equitable and stable economic environment.

A major milestone in stabilising the economy came with the creation of the Federal Reserve under the Federal Reserve Act of 1913. The Federal Reserve, often referred to as "the Fed", was tasked with regulating the money supply and mitigating economic fluctuations. Its establishment marked a pivotal step in addressing the cyclical nature of economic booms and busts.

Social welfare programs also emerged to support vulnerable populations. In 1935, President Franklin D. Roosevelt introduced Social Security as part of his New Deal initiatives. This program provided a safety net for workers, offering retirement pensions to individuals aged sixty-five and older. It aimed to ensure financial stability for retirees, reflecting a significant shift in governmental responsibility toward social welfare.

In 1965, President Lyndon B. Johnson expanded this vision with the creation of Medicare and Medicaid. Medicare provided hospital and medical insurance for older Americans, while Medicaid offered medical coverage for low-income families, individuals with disabilities, those requiring long-term care and pregnant women. These programs became cornerstones of the U.S. social safety net, addressing healthcare access and equity for millions.

These reforms not only addressed immediate economic and social challenges but also laid the foundation for a more resilient and inclusive economic system, shaping the role of government in fostering stability and public welfare. [2]

Beneficiary of World Wars

The U.S. economy received a significant boost during World War I (1914–1918) as the country became a major supplier of goods and weapons to Allied forces while maintaining neutrality until 1917. This period marked the beginning of the U.S.'s transformation into a global economic powerhouse. By capitalising on the demands of war, American industries expanded production and established themselves as key players in international trade and manufacturing.

The 1920s, often referred to as the "Roaring Twenties," further solidified the U.S.'s economic position. The mass production capabilities of American industries, led by innovators like Henry Ford in the auto industry, revolutionised manufacturing and set new benchmarks for efficiency and output. The rise of consumer spending and speculative investments created a climate of economic optimism. However, these euphoric excesses culminated in the stock market crash of October 1929, triggering the Great Depression. This economic downturn, the most severe in U.S. history, saw massive unemployment, widespread bank failures and deflation, leaving the economy in disarray.

The onset of World War II (1939-1945) marked another pivotal moment for the U.S. economy. Mobilising vast labour and industrial resources for military production, the war effort invigorated the American economy and ended the stagnation of the Depression. The U.S.'s dominant role in the Allied victory not only established it as the preeminent military power but also cemented its economic and political leadership in the post-war world.

By 1945, the U.S. emerged as a global leader, with its economy thriving and its influence extending across international political, economic and military domains. This era set the stage for the U.S. to become a central figure in shaping the modern global order. [3]

Post War Boom

The economic growth of the 1950s and 1960s gave rise to a booming middle class and the emergence of a vibrant consumer culture. Suburbanisation became a defining feature of this era, as families moved from city centres to newly developed suburbs. This shift hollowed out urban cores and made automobile commuting a central part of American life. In turn, it bolstered the automobile industry, with companies like General Motors, Ford and Chrysler dominating the U.S. market and becoming household names.

The ideological and geopolitical tensions of the *"Cold War"* further shaped the U.S. economy after World War II. Significant government spending on defense and technology not only secured U.S. military superiority but also spurred economic growth. The production and export of military goods to allied nations became an economic driver, reinforcing the U.S.'s role as a global leader in politics, economics and military.

Technological advancements were another hallmark of this period, driven largely by the dual imperatives of the Space Race and military buildup. The U.S. made substantial investments in research and development, yielding innovations that extended far beyond defense applications. The Apollo 11 mission in 1969, which successfully landed the first humans on the moon, represented a monumental achievement in American ingenuity and technological capability. This accomplishment not only symbolised U.S. dominance in the space race but also further cemented its status as a global leader in economic and political power. [4]. [Study Notes 4]

Stagflation in 1970s

The 1973 OPEC oil embargo, a response to U.S. aid to Israel during the Yom Kippur War, caused oil prices to surge from under USD3 to over USD10 by 1974. Around the same time, the Bretton Woods System was disintegrating and the U.S. faced worsening balance of payments due to the Vietnam War. These overlapping crises led to economic *stagflation; stagnant growth coupled with high inflation*. Meanwhile, the European Economic Community (EEC) and Japan capitalised on the opportunity, experiencing rapid economic growth during this challenging period for the U.S. economy. [5]

In the mid-seventies, families often gathered around black-and-white television sets to watch shows like *The Jack LaLanne Show*. Jack, a renowned fitness guru, led exercises that families tried to follow at home, a simple way to stay entertained when stagflation pinched household budgets. With stagnant wages, spiking oil prices and rising inflation, dining out became a luxury, and household spending on non-essentials plummeted. The economic malaise of stagflation made its presence felt on Main Street, burdening everyday families.

Amidst this gloom came the release of the first ***Star Wars* movie, *Episode IV: A New Hope***. Audiences were introduced to Luke Skywalker as he began his Jedi training with Obi-Wan Kenobi and embarked on a daring mission to rescue Princess Leia and combat the evil Empire. The film offered a symbolic "new hope," lifting spirits during tough times.

As the oil crisis abated and the petrodollar system gained traction, other positive developments emerged. U.S.-China relations normalised, opening China to the world, and the seeds of the technology boom were planted. Meanwhile, *Star Wars* became more than just a blockbuster; it evolved into a cultural phenomenon. Sequels, prequels, iconic characters, and merchandise like Darth Vader costumes and X-Wing Fighter toys permeated global culture.

Economic recovery mirrored the franchise's rise. The *stagflation "Death Star"* was defeated, and like the heroes of *Star Wars*, the U.S. emerged from this dark period with renewed strength. The *Force*, it seemed, was indeed with them.

Technology Boom: the saviour in 1980s to 90s

In the 1980s, President Ronald Reagan introduced tax cuts, deregulation and reduced government spending to stimulate economic growth. This era also saw the rise of the Information Technology (IT) sector, with companies like Microsoft and Apple becoming dominant players. The internet revolution played a pivotal role, transforming the U.S. and global economies. Technological advancements drove sustainable economic growth, shaping the modern digital landscape. [6]

New Frontiers in the 21st Century

The 21st century began with a stock market crash that ended the speculative tech-stock bubble. In 2007, the Global Financial Crisis (GFC) erupted, triggered by subprime mortgages in the U.S. housing market. Unlike typical mortgage lending, which is funded by bank deposits, mortgage banks in the U.S. were able to offer loans backed by funds from investment banks. These investment banks repackaged subprime mortgages into mortgage-backed securities (MBS) and collateralised debt obligations (CDO), which were structured into different tranches with varying risk profiles. These financial products, known collectively as securitised asset-backed securities (ABS), were sold to global investors.

When defaults on subprime mortgages rose due to a downturn in the housing market, panic spread across Wall Street. The resulting exodus from these securities caused their prices to plummet. Financial institutions with leveraged balance sheets could not withstand the impact, leading to the collapse of major U.S. banks like Bear Stearns and Lehman Brothers, both of which disappeared from the financial scene.

(Note: subprime borrowers were people with poor credit-rating history who were unlikely to repay loans.) [7]

	Date or Period	Global Financial Crisis Event
1	15th September 2008	U.S. Bank Lehman Brothers filed for bankruptcy
2	16th September 2008	U.S. Insurance Company AIG received USD 85 billion bailout loan from U.S. Federal Reserve (the "Fed")
3	3rd October 2008	U.S. Congress approves a USD 700 billion bailout package for the U.S. Banks – The Troubled Assets Relief Program (TARP)
4	16th December 2008	The Fed cuts key interest rates to close to zero. The lowest in its 95-year history.

[8]

The COVID-19 pandemic triggered a global economic shutdown, causing a sharp contraction in the U.S. economy and globally. Government stimulus measures, including direct payments and unemployment benefits helped cushion the impact, and the economy rebounded by 2021. In the stock markets, technology stocks soared, driven by the resilience of their business models and super-low interest rates from the global financial crisis. Companies like Facebook (now Meta), Amazon, Apple, Netflix and Google, known as "FAANG" stocks, became the dominant players in the market. In 2023, the rise of Artificial Intelligence sparked a new frenzy, with stocks like Nvidia emerging as market darlings. The herd mentality and animal instincts continue to shape the stock market, highlighting the difficulty in controlling the ebb and flow of international capital. Economic cycles, though challenging, have become a natural market phenomenon.

Through these successes and failures, the U.S. economy underwent numerous reforms aimed at protecting consumers, regulating markets and fostering technological development. Despite economic downturns, the U.S. economy demonstrated resilience, bouncing back each time. These cycles of demand and supply in the USD have helped maintain the USD's status as the world's reserve currency into the 21st century.

ECONOMIC CRISIS MANAGEMENT

The Global Financial Crisis (GFC) led to the introduction of an unconventional monetary policy tool: ***Quantitative Easing (QE)***. This tool was used by central banks to stimulate the economy when standard monetary policies, such as lowering short term interest rates became ineffective especially when such rates were already near zero. Under QE, central banks purchase long-term securities, such as government bonds, mortgage-backed securities and sometimes corporate bonds from the open market. This increases the money supply and encourages lending and investment.

Quantitative Easing (QE)

Central banks, such as the U.S. Federal Reserve, purchase financial assets like government bonds from commercial banks and other financial institutions. Specifically, the Fed buys longer-maturity securities to lower long-term yields, creating a flatter yield curve (*a visual representation of interest rates on U.S. Treasuries of varying maturities*). The goal is to narrow the gap between short-term and long-term rates, stimulating longer-term borrowing and lending. This policy is a form of "Yield Curve Control," also implemented by the Bank of Japan (BOJ) to fight deflation.

By crediting financial institutions' accounts, the central bank increases the reserves in the banking system. This raises the demand for bonds, which drives up their prices and lowers interest rates. With reduced borrowing costs, businesses are encouraged to invest, expand and hire, while consumers are more likely to spend. The aim is to boost economic activity and prevent deflation. However, the effectiveness of QE depends on rational human behaviour, assuming it leads to the desired increase in investment and consumption.

How the Fed "Prints Money" Electronically

In essence, the Fed electronically "prints" money by purchasing securities from commercial banks, crediting them with new reserves. This increases the money supply without physically printing currency. The central bank's balance sheet expands as it acquires more U.S. Treasury securities (USTs) and the commercial banks' balance sheets reflect an increase in cash reserves. After this electronic "money printing" process, it is up to the discretion of the banks and financial institutions to lend out the new money to stimulate the economy.

Before Quantitative Easing (QE) induced "electronic money printing"

Before the Federal Reserve initiates Quantitative Easing (QE), its balance sheet typically includes assets such as U.S. Treasury securities (USTs), with corresponding liabilities representing money in circulation.

F1: Fed's Balance Sheet

Assets:	Liabilities:
$100 (USTs government bonds)	$100 (currency circulating in the economy)
	Money circulating in the economy

B1: Bank's Balance Sheet

Assets:	Liabilities:
$2000 (USTs purchased from market)	$2000 (client deposits in bank accounts)

No New monies created before QE

After Quantitative Easing (QE) induced "electronic money printing"

When QE is implemented, the Fed buys additional USTs (U.S. Treasuries), increasing its assets. To balance the books, the Fed credits the commercial banking system with the equivalent amount of new money, increasing the money supply.

F2: Fed's Balance Sheet

Assets:	Liabilities:
$100 (USTs government bonds)	$100 (currency circulating in the economy)
$1000 New USTs purchased via QE	***$1000 new Money created and injected into banking system***

B2: Bank's Balance Sheet (After QE)

Assets:	Liabilities:
$1000 (USTs after sale of $1000 to Fed)	$2000 (client deposits in bank accounts)
$1000 cash added to bank,	*Deposits remain unchanged*

New monies surfaces at bank after QE

Global Financial Crisis 2007-2009

During the Global Financial Crisis (GFC), the Federal Reserve and other central banks around the world implemented *Quantitative Easing (QE)* to combat the severe economic downturn. Short term Interest rates were already near zero, leaving QE as one of the few remaining options to stimulate the economy. The U.S. Federal Reserve, launched several rounds of QE, known as QE1-2008, QE2-2010 and QE3-2012. [9]

Primary Effects of Quantitative Easing (QE)

One of the primary effects of QE is the reduction of long-term interest rates. When the central bank purchases long-term government bonds and other fixed-income assets, it drives up their prices, which in turn lowers their yields or interest rates. This makes borrowing cheaper for both businesses and consumers, encouraging spending, investment and ultimately boosting economic growth.

As these lower yields make bonds less attractive, investors are often driven to seek higher returns in riskier assets such as equities and corporate bonds, which pushes up their prices. This rise in asset prices can create what is known as the ***"wealth effect"***, where individuals feel wealthier due to the increased value of their financial holdings, leading them to spend more. However, this wealth effect is not evenly distributed. Wealthier individuals who own more financial assets are the primary beneficiaries, while those who do not have significant investments in stocks or bonds may not experience the same gains.

Another significant impact is on the housing market. QE lowers mortgage rates, making home loans more affordable and thus stimulating demand in the housing market. While this benefits current homeowners by increasing the value of their properties, it can also make housing less affordable for first-time buyers, further exacerbating inequality.

In addition, QE acts as a signal to markets that the central bank is committed to supporting the economy. This can boost confidence among investors, businesses and consumers, encouraging more spending and investment, which helps stabilise financial markets. During periods of crisis, like the Global Financial Crisis, QE also plays a critical role in preventing deflation, a general decline in prices that can lead to reduced consumer spending, higher real debt burdens and economic stagnation. By increasing the money supply and promoting spending, QE helps stabilise prices and avert a deflationary spiral.

Secondary Effects of Quantitative Easing (QE)

While QE can stimulate economic growth, it can also have secondary effects, particularly in contributing to *widening income* and *wealth inequality*. Since QE drives up the prices of financial assets, those who already own these assets, typically wealthier individuals, benefit the most. Meanwhile, wage growth and improvements in the wider economy take longer to reach lower-income individuals. As a result, the wealth gap between the rich and the rest of society can increase.

Lastly, QE often leads to *currency depreciation*. As the central bank increases the money supply, foreign investors may seek higher returns elsewhere, leading to a weaker currency. While a depreciated currency can make exports cheaper and more competitive on the global market, it can also create trade imbalances by mispricing exported goods. Moreover, it may provoke tensions with other countries that view such currency depreciation as a form of competitive devaluation, potentially leading to friction in international trade relations.

In conclusion, while QE can provide short-term economic stimulus and help prevent deflation, it also has significant side effects, particularly in terms of income inequality, housing affordability and currency depreciation.

Risk-Taking and Potential Asset Bubbles

Quantitative Easing (QE) can *incentivise riskier behaviour* in financial markets. With interest rates at near-zero levels, investors often seek higher returns by shifting into riskier assets, such as junk bonds, emerging market debt or speculative real estate. This can lead to the *creation of asset bubbles*, where the surge in asset prices becomes unsustainable, as seen in the dot-com bubble and the housing bubble. While QE played a crucial role in stabilising the economy during the financial crisis, concerns arose that it might set the stage for future asset price bubbles.

On the other hand, unwinding QE, referred to as Quantitative Tightening (QT), has proven to be difficult. The U.S. Federal Reserve's massive balance sheet requires a careful and gradual unwind process to avoid triggering another shock to the financial system. If not done systematically and in an orderly manner, such an offload of assets can undo the stabilising effects that QE aims to achieve, potentially causing market instability.

Distortion of Financial Markets

Long-term use of Quantitative Easing (QE) can distort financial markets by artificially lowering yields. When central banks implement continuous QE programs, they suppress bond yields *(the implied interest rate of bonds)* to levels that may not accurately reflect the true risk of lending. This distorts the real price of debt and *can encourage excessive borrowing*. Over time, markets may become overly reliant on central bank intervention by assuming QE will continue indefinitely. When central banks begin to unwind these programmes, it can lead to market volatility.

A notable example of how such distortions can trigger instability is the collapse of *Silicon Valley Bank (SVB) in March 2023*. SVB had total assets amounting to approximately USD 200 billion before its failure. The bank benefited during the tech boom and venture capital (VC) upcycle when large deposits flowed in. However, when the Federal Reserve began raising interest rates rapidly after the COVID-19 pandemic, SVB's management was caught off guard. The bank held long-term fixed income assets that were unhedged against interest rate risk, causing a significant fall in the value of these assets.

If the bank had to sell these assets to meet withdrawal demands, it would have realised a loss. As depositors, particularly from tech companies and VCs, rushed to withdraw their funds, the proceeds from asset sales were insufficient to cover the demands. This led to a panic-driven bank run. SVB's collapse highlights a failure in risk management, where the distortion of asset prices due to QE, combined with laxity in managing interest rate risk, contributed to the bank's demise. [10]

Potential for Inflation

Although Quantitative Easing (QE) is designed to combat deflation, it carries the risk of eventually leading to inflation. As QE injects more money into the economy, if the growth in the money supply outpaces the economy's ability to produce goods and services, it can result in rising prices. This happens because there would be more "paper money" chasing fewer goods and services.

In the immediate aftermath of the Global Financial Crisis (GFC), inflation remained low due to weak demand. However, there were concerns that prolonged QE, if combined with a rapid pickup in economic activity, could eventually trigger inflation. As the economy recovers and demand increases, the excess money supply could lead to upward pressure on prices, creating an inflationary environment.

After the Global Financial Crisis

After the initial rounds of QE in response to the GFC, central banks, especially the Federal Reserve, continued using QE during later periods of economic stress. In 2020, during the COVID-19 pandemic, the Fed and other central banks launched even larger rounds of QE to stabilise financial markets and support economies through lockdowns and the sharp decline in economic activity. The Fed's balance sheet expanded dramatically as it purchased government bonds and mortgage-backed securities on an unprecedented scale.

As the global economy began to recover from the pandemic, concerns over inflation grew due to the large-scale QE programs, supply chain disruptions and pent-up demand. By 2022 and 2023, inflationary pressures became more pronounced, prompting central banks to consider tapering QE and raising interest rates to combat rising prices and stabilise inflation.

Addicted to Quantitative Easing (QE)

QE was a key tool used during the Global Financial Crisis to stabilise the economy, lower interest rates and prevent deflation. Its primary effects included reduced borrowing costs, higher asset prices and increased confidence, all of which helped to revive economic growth. However, QE also had secondary effects, such as contributing to wealth inequality, encouraging risk-taking and potentially distorting financial markets. In the long term, QE remains a controversial policy, particularly due to its potential to fuel inflation and create imbalances in financial markets.

TWIN DEFICITS: THE ELEPHANT IN THE ROOM

The U.S. Current Account and Trade Account are key components of the country's balance of payments, tracking economic transactions between the U.S. and the rest of the world. These accounts are intrinsically linked to the concept of "twin deficits," which refers to the simultaneous occurrence of a government budget deficit and a trade-related current account deficit.

To understand this better, imagine Mary, who has a checking account at ACME Bank. Mary spends more than her monthly income, running a deficit in her account. To cover this shortfall, she either dips into her savings or borrows from her credit line. If she continues to overspend without addressing her deficit, her balance grows increasingly negative. Eventually, the bank may refuse further transactions, demanding repayment.

Now, think of Mary's checking account as the U.S. current account, which tracks the flow of money through exports, imports and investments. If the U.S. imports more than it exports, it runs a trade deficit, just as Mary spends beyond her income. Similarly, if the U.S. government spends more than it collects in revenue, it runs a budget deficit, like Mary's overspending. When both these deficits occur together, they form what economists call "twin deficits."

However, unlike Mary, the U.S. has a unique advantage: it issues the world's reserve currency, the USD. This allows the U.S. to borrow by issuing Treasury bonds, which are purchased globally due to the demand for USD-denominated assets. The Federal Reserve can also print money to fund deficits. This privileged position shields the U.S. from immediate consequences, but persistent deficits raise concerns about long-term fiscal sustainability.

COMPONENTS OF THE CURRENT ACCOUNT

The U.S. current account reflects whether the country is a net lender or borrower to the world. A deficit means the U.S. is borrowing to finance its consumption and investments. The current account comprises the following:

- ✓ **Goods Trade** includes tangible products like automobiles, electronics and oil. The U.S. consistently runs a deficit here due to high consumer demand for imports and the offshoring of manufacturing.
- ✓ **Services Trade** covers intangible services like financial services, tourism and technology. The U.S. typically runs a surplus, exporting more services than it imports.
- ✓ **Primary Income** tracks income earned by U.S. citizens from abroad and payments to foreign investors, such as interest or dividends.
- ✓ **Secondary Income** includes remittances, foreign aid and other unilateral transfers like gifts or donations.

THE TRADE BALANCE

The trade balance, comprising goods and services can result in a *surplus (exports exceed imports)* or a *deficit (imports exceed exports)*. While the U.S. runs surpluses in services, this is outweighed by its goods deficit.

HOW TWIN DEFICITS CAME TO BE

The *"twin deficits"* phenomenon in the U.S. arises from the interplay between:
- ✓ **The Fiscal Deficit** which occurs when government spending exceeds revenue, leading to borrowing via Treasury bonds. Persistent fiscal deficits increase national debt.

✓ **The Current Account Deficit** which results when imports of goods, services and capital exceed exports, requiring foreign investments to finance the shortfall.

HOW FISCAL DEFICITS WORSEN CURRENT ACCOUNT DEFICITS

Returning to Mary, imagine she continues overspending while borrowing from friends. To attract these loans, she promises high returns or offers attractive terms. Similarly, when the U.S. government runs fiscal deficits, it borrows by issuing Treasury bonds. If domestic savings are insufficient, it turns to foreign investors. As foreign investors buy U.S. assets, demand for the U.S. Dollar rises, strengthening its value. A stronger dollar makes U.S. exports costlier and imports cheaper, worsening the trade deficit. This creates a cycle where fiscal deficits and current account deficits reinforce each other, *solidifying the "twin deficits"*.

RISKS OF TWIN DEFICITS

While the U.S. enjoys the unique advantage of issuing the world's reserve currency, this privilege comes with inherent risks. Persistent fiscal and current account deficits depend on a steady global demand for USD-denominated assets. Should key creditors like China or Japan scale back their investments or if confidence in the USD diminishes, the U.S. economy could face significant repercussions.

A loss of global appetite for U.S. Treasuries or the U.S. Dollar would likely trigger capital outflows, leading to a sharp depreciation of the USD, higher borrowing costs and a destabilised financial system. The result would resemble Mary's overspending and unchecked borrowing, an unsustainable pattern that eventually collapses under its own weight.

The critical question is: how long can the global economy continue to sustain these imbalances before seeking alternatives? [12]

IMPLICATIONS OF TWIN DEFICITS

The twin deficits comprising the fiscal deficit and current account deficit have placed the U.S. in a position of heavy reliance on foreign capital. Countries like China, Japan and Saudi Arabia have historically purchased significant amounts of U.S. Treasury bonds, indirectly funding U.S. government spending and trade imbalances.

However, this dependency creates vulnerabilities. If foreign investors lose confidence in the U.S.'s fiscal discipline or its ability to manage debt, the consequences could be severe. A sharp reduction in foreign investment would likely lead to a depreciation of the U.S. Dollar, increasing inflationary pressures and borrowing costs while destabilising financial markets.

The twin deficits are not merely an economic imbalance, they reflect a system overly reliant on foreign support. Unless addressed through strategic reforms, this model could erode the U.S.'s economic dominance and financial stability in the long run.

Just as Mary faces financial instability when her spending far exceeds her income, the U.S. risks similar vulnerabilities. The global economy may continue financing these imbalances for now, but the sustainability of this arrangement is increasingly under question. Addressing the twin deficits is essential to ensuring long-term economic resilience and safeguarding the U.S.'s position in the global financial system.

EVOLUTION OF TWIN DEFICITS

1980s witnessed the birth of the Twin Deficits: the concept of twin deficits came to prominence in the 1980s under the administration of President Ronald Reagan. Reaganomics, which involved significant tax cuts and increased defence spending, led to a large federal budget deficit. Meanwhile, monetary policy focused on reducing inflation which resulted in high interest rates and attracted foreign capital. The influx of foreign capital appreciated the USD, making exports less competitive and increasing imports, which led to a growing current account deficit.

1990s: Temporary decline. In the late 1990s, under President Bill Clinton, the U.S. saw a budget surplus (driven by higher tax revenues from the booming economy and tech sector), and the current account deficit temporarily narrowed. However, the current account deficit persisted because of continued high demand for imports and capital inflows.

2000s: Widening and got worse. The early 2000s saw the return of both large fiscal and current account deficits. Tax cuts under President George W. Bush and increased military spending after 9/11 (Iraq and Afghanistan wars) led to rising federal deficits. The housing boom, financed by foreign capital inflows, further contributed to the widening current account deficit. The current account deficit peaked in 2006 at about 6% of GDP.

2007-2009: Global Financial Crisis. The financial crisis led to a reduction in both deficits as trade and investment slowed during the recession. However, the fiscal deficit ballooned due to stimulus spending and bailouts aimed at stabilising the economy.

2010-2024: Cracks begin to show. In the aftermath of the crisis, the current account deficit remained lower than its mid-2000s peak but continued to fluctuate. The fiscal deficit remained elevated due to continued government spending and tax policies, including the 2017 Tax Cuts and Jobs Act. In the 2020s, the COVID-19 pandemic led to a sharp increase in the fiscal deficit as the government spent trillions on relief programs, and the current account deficit widened due to the global economic downturn and trade disruptions.

BALLOONING DEBT

The ballooning U.S. national debt is the result of decades of government spending outpacing revenue, leading to persistent budget deficits. Various factors, including increased domestic and international spending, have contributed to the sharp rise in debt. Below is a breakdown of how government spending, both domestic and foreign, has driven the rise in U.S. debt, alongside key historical events that exacerbated this trend.

Understanding the U.S. National Debt: The U.S. national debt consists of the total amount of money the federal government owes to its creditors, including domestic and foreign entities. It grows when the government runs a budget deficit, meaning annual spending exceeds revenue. The government finances this deficit by borrowing, mainly through the issuance of U.S. Treasury bonds. **Gross National Debt:** As of 2024, the U.S. national debt is over $33 trillion. (See Figure 4a) **Debt-to-GDP Ratio:** the debt is often measured as a percentage of Gross Domestic Product GDP, with the debt-to-GDP ratio nearing or exceeding 100%, indicating that the total debt is roughly equal to the entire economy's annual output. [12]

The Elephant in the Room

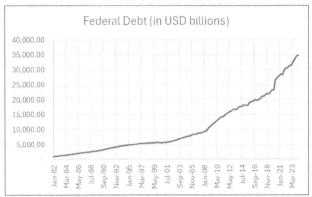
U.S. Department of Treasury, Fiscal Service

Figure 4a: *U.S. Federal Debt*

Key Drivers of U.S. Debt Growth are **Domestic Spending** and **Military Spending**. In domestic spending, major *social entitlement programs* such as Social Security, Medicare and Medicaid account for a significant portion of federal spending. *Social Security* provides income for retirees, the disabled and survivors of deceased workers. As the U.S. population ages, spending on Social Security has increased significantly. *Medicare and Medicaid* provide health care for seniors, while Medicaid supports low-income individuals. Rising health care costs and the aging population have made these programmes major contributors to the deficit. *Public Welfare*: government spending on programmes like unemployment insurance, food assistance and housing support expanded significantly during economic downturns, particularly after the 2008 financial crisis and the COVID-19 pandemic.

In *Defence and Military Spending*, the U.S. has historically maintained a large defence budget, accounting for a significant portion of federal spending. During the Cold War and in the post-9/11 era, defence spending increased due to conflicts like the wars in Afghanistan and Iraq, as well as efforts to maintain global military presence. Defence spending rose during the Reagan administration (1980s) as part of a military buildup against the Soviet Union. Post-2001, military spending spiked due to the War on Terror, including operations in Afghanistan and Iraq, as well as investments in defence technology.

Interest on the Debt: As the national debt grows, the government must pay interest on the borrowed money. Interest payments are one of the fastest-growing components of the federal budget. As of 2024, with rising interest rates, within a decade, the cost of servicing the debt is expected to exceed key domestic programmes.

Tax Policies and Revenue Shortfalls: In addition to spending, tax policies play a crucial role in the growth of the national debt. Key tax cuts throughout U.S. history have reduced government revenue while spending has continued to grow. The *Bush Tax Cuts* in 2001 and 2003 significantly reduced revenue, contributing to the growing deficit, especially as they coincided with wars in Afghanistan and Iraq. *Trump Tax Cuts and Jobs Act* in 2017 lowered corporate and individual tax rates. While proponents argued it would spur economic growth, it led to a significant reduction in government revenue, contributing to annual budget deficits. [13]

Growing Entitlement Spending: As the U.S. population ages, spending on entitlement programs like Social Security and Medicare has surged. **Aging Population:** The large baby boomer generation has been retiring, putting strain on the Social Security and Medicare systems as more people become eligible for benefits and as health care costs rise. **Healthcare Costs:** The cost of health care in the U.S. has risen dramatically, increasing the federal government's expenditure to cover Medicare and Medicaid expenditures.

DEBT GROWTH HISTORY

Reaganomics
Tax Cuts: President Ronald Reagan implemented significant tax cuts under Reaganomics, based on supply-side economic theory, which posited that lower taxes would stimulate economic growth. However, these tax cuts also significantly reduced federal revenue. Defence buildup and military spending soared during the Cold War as the U.S. sought to counter Soviet power. This increase in defence spending, combined with tax cuts, caused the national debt to nearly triple by the end of the Reagan administration.

9/11 and the War on Terror
After the 9/11 attacks, President George W. Bush led the U.S. into wars in Afghanistan (2001) and Iraq (2003). These long-term military engagements, along with heightened homeland security spending, added trillions to the national debt. Bush tax cuts of 2001 and 2003 reduced federal revenue while spending increased, contributing to a rise in deficits.

Global Financial Crisis
The Great Recession led to a sharp increase in government spending as the economy contracted. Government spending rose on social safety net programs like unemployment benefits, while revenues fell due to lower tax collections. Stimulus Programs in 2009, saw President Barack Obama signed the American Recovery and Reinvestment Act (ARRA), a $787 billion stimulus package designed to jumpstart the economy. This further increased the deficit.

COVID-19 Pandemic
The COVID-19 pandemic caused the U.S. government to spend unprecedented amounts to address both the public health crisis and its economic fallout. Programmes like the CARES Act (over $2 trillion) and subsequent relief bills provided stimulus checks, expanded unemployment benefits, support for businesses, state governments and health care. The national debt grew by $3.7 trillion in 2020 alone, marking one of the largest single-year increases in U.S. history. The pandemic also caused a significant drop in tax revenue as businesses shut down, unemployment soared and the economy slowed. [14]

Long-Term Consequences of Ballooning Debt would firstly increase *Interest Burden.* Rising debt levels mean the U.S. government is spending more just to service its debt, leaving less for productive investments like infrastructure, education and research. Secondly, the *Crowding Out* effect creeps in. High government borrowing can lead to higher interest rates, which may crowd out private investment, slowing long-term economic growth. Thirdly, the economy becomes *susceptible to crisis.* Although the U.S. can currently borrow at relatively low rates due to its status as the world's reserve currency issuer, sustained deficits and debt could eventually lead to a loss of investor confidence, resulting in higher borrowing costs or even a debt crisis.

Bursting the debt Balloon

The ballooning U.S. debt is the product of decades of persistent government spending which has exceeded revenues. Key drivers include large-scale military expenditures, expanding entitlement programs and the economic impact of crises like the Global Financial Crisis and the COVID-19 pandemic. While government spending has been necessary for certain priorities, such as social programmes and economic recovery, the lack of offsetting revenue has led to growing deficits and a rising national debt that poses significant long-term challenges.

UNITED STATES FEDERAL RESERVE

The Federal Reserve (commonly referred to as the Fed) is the central bank of the United States and plays a critical role in the country's economy through its conduct of monetary policy. The Fed's actions influence inflation, employment, interest rates and overall economic stability. This section provides a detailed explanation of the Federal Reserve's role, how it conducts monetary policy, its dual mandate, and the role of the Federal Open Market Committee (FOMC).

The Federal Reserve was established in 1913 with the signing of the Federal Reserve Act, in response to financial panics and banking instability. It has since evolved into a central institution tasked with promoting economic stability and addressing various financial challenges.

The Fed's Primary Roles are to conduct monetary policy, influence the availability of money and credit to promote a stable economy, supervise and regulate banks, ensure the safety and soundness of the banking system, protect consumers, maintain financial stability, act as a lender of last resort to prevent financial crises and finally, to facilitate an efficient and secure payment system, including clearing checks and electronic payments.

The Federal Reserve's Dual Mandate was set by Congress in 1977 as part of the Federal Reserve Reform Act. The first of the dual mandate instructs the Fed to *Promote Maximum Employment.* This involves striving for full employment or the highest level of employment that the economy can sustain without causing excessive inflation. The second of the dual mandate is to *Ensure Price Stability.* This requires keeping inflation at a low and stable rate. The Fed aims for an average inflation rate of 2% over time, using the Personal Consumption Expenditures (PCE) price index as its preferred measure. The balance between these two objectives: maximising employment and stabilising prices guides the Fed's monetary policy decisions. Sometimes these goals conflict, for example, when reducing inflation could slow down economic growth and increase unemployment. The Fed must navigate these trade-offs carefully.

Federal Reserve Conduct of Monetary Policy

The Fed conducts monetary policy primarily through three key tools, which influence interest rates and the overall money supply in the economy:

Open Market Operations (OMOs) is the most used tool of monetary policy and involves the buying and selling of U.S. Treasury securities in the open market. When the Fed buys government bonds from banks and financial institutions, it injects money into the banking system, increasing the money supply and lowering interest rates. This encourages borrowing, investment and consumption, stimulating the economy. Conversely, when the Fed sells bonds, it removes money from the banking system, decreasing the money supply and raising interest rates. This discourages borrowing and spending, cooling down an overheating economy.

Discount Rate is the interest rate the Fed charges commercial banks for short-term loans through the discount window. *Lowering the Discount Rate* makes borrowing from the Fed cheaper for banks, encouraging them to lend more to consumers and businesses, thus expanding economic activity. *Raising the Discount Rate* makes borrowing from the Fed more expensive, leading banks to lend less, slowing down the economy. **Reserve Requirements** is the portion of customer deposits that banks are required to hold in reserve and not lend out. By *lowering reserve requirements*, the Fed allows banks to lend out more of their deposits, increasing the money supply and stimulating economic activity. By *raising reserve requirements*, the Fed limits the amount banks can lend, reducing the money supply and slowing down the economy.

Interest on Excess Reserves (IOER) is a tool introduced after the 2008 financial crisis, allowing the Fed to pay interest on excess reserves held by banks at the central bank. *Raising IOER* means the Fed pays higher interest on excess reserves, encouraging banks to keep more money at the central bank rather than lending it out, tightening monetary conditions. *Lowering IOER* works in the opposite way, encouraging banks to lend more, increasing the money supply and stimulating economic growth.

The Federal Open Market Committee (FOMC) is the body within the Federal Reserve that is responsible for overseeing open market operations (the buying and selling of U.S. Treasury securities) and setting interest rates. The FOMC plays a central role in the formulation of monetary policy. The FOMC consists of 12 voting members. Seven are members of the Federal Reserve Board of Governors, who are appointed by the President and confirmed by the Senate. Another is the President of the Federal Reserve Bank of New York who permanently holds a voting seat due to the New York Fed's role in executing open market operations. The remaining four are presidents of the 11 other regional Federal Reserve Banks, who are rotated annually as voting members. All 12 regional bank presidents participate in FOMC discussions, but only five (including the New York Fed president) have a vote at any given time. The FOMC meets eight times a year (approximately every six weeks) to assess the state of the U.S. economy and make decisions on monetary policy. These decisions are primarily focused on setting the federal funds rate and guiding expectations for future interest rate adjustments.

Federal Funds Rate is the interest rate at which banks lend reserves to each other overnight. The Fed influences this rate through its open market operations, and it serves as a benchmark for other interest rates in the economy, such as mortgage and business loan rates. In addition to changing interest rates, the Fed often provides forward guidance, which signals its expectations for future monetary policy. This helps influence market expectations and economic behaviour. [15]

The Federal Reserve's Response to Crises

The Fed's role becomes especially critical during economic crises when it must act decisively to stabilise the financial system and restore economic growth. Two recent examples of crises responses highlight its importance:
During **Global Financial Crisis 2007-2009,** the Federal Reserve deployed several unconventional monetary policy tools to stabilise the economy, in addition to its traditional tools.
Quantitative Easing QE: The Fed purchased large amounts of government bonds and mortgage-backed securities to lower long-term interest rates and inject liquidity into the financial system.
Near-Zero Interest Rates: The FOMC lowered the federal funds rate to near-zero levels (0-0.25%) to encourage borrowing and investment.
Lending Facilities: The Fed set up various emergency lending facilities to provide liquidity to banks, businesses and even municipalities to prevent a collapse of the financial system.

COVID-19 Pandemic 2020
The Federal Reserve took swift action in response to the economic disruption caused by the COVID-19 pandemic:
Aggressive QE: The Fed launched another large-scale QE program, purchasing trillions of dollars in U.S. Treasuries and mortgage-backed securities.
Interest Rate Cuts: The Fed slashed the federal funds rate to near-zero again.
Lending Programs: The Fed set up programmes to support small businesses (via the Main Street Lending Program), municipalities and corporate debt markets, ensuring credit flow even in the face of an economic shutdown.

Challenges and Criticisms of the Federal Reserve's Monetary Policies
The Federal Reserve has faced several challenges and criticisms related to its conduct of monetary policy:
Inflation Control: While the Fed has been successful at keeping inflation low over much of its history, there are concerns that prolonged low interest rates and large QE programme can lead to inflationary pressures. In 2021 and 2022, rising inflation became a significant concern, forcing the Fed to adjust its policies.
Financial Stability: Some argue that the Fed's policies, especially low interest rates and QE, contribute to asset bubbles (e.g., stock markets and real estate) by pushing investors into riskier assets in search of higher returns.
Income Inequality: Critics argue that the Fed's policies, particularly QE, disproportionately benefit wealthier individuals and corporations by inflating asset prices (stocks, bonds and real estate), which wealthier households are more likely to own.
Policy Lag: Monetary policy can take time to work its way through the economy. This lag makes it difficult for the Fed to time its interventions perfectly and therefore, policy changes may come too late or be too aggressive.

THE FED TO THE RESCUE

The Federal Reserve, through its mandate of promoting maximum employment and price stability, plays a crucial role in maintaining U.S. economic stability. Its main tool for influencing the economy is monetary policy, conducted primarily through the actions of the FOMC. By adjusting interest rates, buying or selling government securities and providing forward guidance, the Fed seeks to manage inflation and support employment.

In times of crises, the Fed's ability to act as a lender of last resort and use unconventional tools like quantitative easing has proven critical in stabilising financial markets and the broader economy. However, its policies also come with trade-offs and its decisions are often the subject of debate.

In practice, more money was being circulated in the financial system under QE. Basic economics 101 tells us that if supply of a good (in this case USD) increases, the price of this good will fall. And since there are now more USD notes in circulation under QE chasing after the same goods and services, the prices of goods and services will have to increase. This is how inflation appears to erode our purchasing power. If inflation rears its ugly head, interest rates will have to increase to reign in prices. Buyers of U.S. Treasuries may hesitate to increase their U.S. Treasury (UST) holdings as the increased printing of USD notes would debase the value of USD leading to its depreciation against other currencies, rendering UST less attractive of an asset to hold. Fed's continued effort to rescue the U.S. economy and implicitly USD may become increasingly onerous.

Chapter 5
Tremors, More Tremors and Continued Audacity
The increasing geopolitical tensions involving the U.S., its economic woes creating global tremors felt by nervous trading partners, showing signs of cracks in the USD's reserve currency status

The USD has long been the backbone of global trade and finance, its strength derived from the size of the U.S. economy, the depth of its financial markets and widespread trust in its institutions.

However, between 2000 and 2024, several events have tested its credibility, sparking debates about its future as the world's dominant reserve currency.

For decades, the USD has facilitated international transactions, provided liquidity and served as a stable store of value. Its centrality in global trade and financial systems cemented its position as the primary reserve currency. Yet, cracks have started to appear.

The weaponisation of the USD through sanctions has driven countries like China and Russia to seek alternatives. Rising U.S. debt and monetary policies, such as quantitative easing after the 2008 financial crisis, have raised concerns about inflation and the USD's stability. Geopolitical tensions, including trade disputes with China, have further accelerated efforts to reduce reliance on the dollar, with emerging systems like BRICS initiatives and digital currencies offering potential alternatives.

The USD's role as a global reserve is also being questioned due to perceived bias in U.S. policy decisions, which prioritise domestic interests over global stability. While over 58% of global reserves were still held in USD as of 2023, there is a clear trend of diversification as nations increasingly look to gold, regional currencies and bilateral trade agreements to hedge against volatility.

As the lyrics from *The Sound of Music* suggest, grappling with the USD's evolving role is like trying to *"catch a cloud and pin it down"*. While the USD's decline as the world's reserve currency is not imminent, the rise of a multipolar currency system signals a slow but steady shift. The USD's future will depend on the U.S.'s ability to balance domestic priorities with its global responsibilities, ensuring it remains a trusted and stable cornerstone of international finance.

POLITICAL TREMORS

Could the evolving geopolitical developments of the early 21st century hasten the demise of the USD or on the contrary, reinforce her premier status?

AFGHAN AND IRAQI WARS
The U.S. invasions of Afghanistan in 2001 and Iraq in 2003 marked the beginning of costly and controversial wars that shaped the early 21st century. The Afghanistan invasion was a direct response to the 9/11 attacks, as the Taliban regime refused to surrender Osama bin Laden, the mastermind behind the tragedy. In Iraq, the U.S.-led coalition sought to eliminate supposed weapons of mass destruction (WMDs) and end Saddam Hussein's oppressive rule. However, no WMDs were ever found, raising questions about the war's legitimacy.

These conflicts carried enormous financial and political costs. With expenditures exceeding USD 2 trillion, they significantly contributed to the U.S.'s rising budget deficits and national debt. The wars also dented global perceptions of U.S. leadership, with critics citing flawed intelligence and strategic miscalculations.

Together, the Afghan and Iraqi wars highlighted the complexities and consequences of military intervention, leaving a lasting impact on U.S. foreign policy, global stability and economic priorities.

RUSSIAN UKRAINE WAR

In February 2022, Russia launched an invasion of Ukraine, framing it as a "special military operation" to support the self-proclaimed Republics of Donetsk and Luhansk, whose paramilitary forces had been engaged in conflict with Ukraine since 2014. In response, the U.S. led a global coalition to support Ukraine's defence, aiming to uphold Ukraine's sovereignty while imposing severe economic sanctions on Russia to deter further aggression.

The U.S. sanctions targeted key sectors of the Russian economy, including energy, banking and defence, while also freezing or confiscating Russian assets, many of which were denominated in USD. Some of these funds were reportedly repurposed to finance aid to Ukraine. Alongside its allies, as well as the IMF and World Bank, the U.S. committed over USD 75 billion in aid, encompassing humanitarian assistance, military equipment, ammunition and funding for essential Ukrainian services.

This coordinated effort sought not only to bolster Ukraine's resistance but also to cripple Russia's ability to sustain its military campaign, showcasing the dual role of the USD as both an instrument of economic power and a facilitator of global aid.

EROSION OF TRUST

U.S. foreign policy decisions, particularly the Iraq War, drew significant international criticism, even from key allies, due to its perceived lack of justification. This scepticism undermined global confidence in U.S. leadership, fostering doubts about its judgment and consistency on the world stage.

While these controversies did not immediately threaten the dominance of the USD, they highlighted vulnerabilities tied to U.S. political credibility. Financing costly wars such as Iraq and Afghanistan substantially increased its national debt, raising long-term concerns about the sustainability of the USD's role as the global reserve currency. This erosion of trust, coupled with mounting fiscal challenges, has sparked debates over the future stability of the USD's position in global finance.

ECONOMIC TREMORS

GLOBAL FINANCIAL CRISIS (GFC)

The Global Financial Crisis (GFC), beginning in 2007, was a pivotal event that shook global confidence in the U.S. economy and financial system. It exposed systemic vulnerabilities within U.S. financial markets, undermining trust in the USD's reliability as the world's reserve currency. The collapse of major financial institutions like Lehman Brothers and Bear Stearns, coupled with the bailout of AIG, highlighted these risks and triggered a global recession. Ironically, the USD strengthened during the crisis due to its "safe haven" status, despite its association with the turmoil.

The Federal Reserve's response, particularly the implementation of Quantitative Easing (QE), added longer-term concerns. By purchasing large volumes of U.S. Treasury bonds (USTs) and mortgage-backed securities (MBSs), (see Chapter 2 [Box 2A]) the Fed injected substantial liquidity into the economy. While this stabilised markets in the short term, critics argue it increased the money supply *(through the electronic printing of money)* significantly, raising fears of inflation and USD losing its value. Although inflation remained subdued immediately post-crisis, scepticism about the future value of the USD lingered.

TRADE WARS AND PROTECTIONISM

The trade war initiated by the Trump administration in 2018 further complicated the USD's standing. Reciprocal tariffs between the U.S. and China not only strained economic ties but also incentivised some countries to diversify away from the USD in trade and reserves. At the same time, China's Belt and Road Initiative (BRI) encouraged the use of the Chinese yuan (RMB) in international trade, subtly eroding the USD's dominance in certain regions.

GLOBAL REACTIONS TO U.S. SANCTIONS

The U.S.'s frequent use of economic sanctions against countries like Iran, Russia and Venezuela also motivated those nations to seek alternatives to the USD. For example, Russia and China increasingly settled bilateral trade agreements using local currencies rather than the USD, including in crude oil transactions.

DE-DOLLARISATION EFFORTS

Efforts to "de-dollarise" gained momentum in response to these events. Nations like Russia and China have promoted alternative currencies, such as the EUR, Chinese RMB, and digital currencies, for trade and reserve purposes. This trend has been particularly evident in the energy sector, where non-USD settlements for oil transactions have gained traction. These de-dollarisation efforts, while not yet displacing the USD, signal a gradual shift in the global financial system and reflect diminishing reliance on the USD in certain regions and industries.

DOMESTIC TREMORS

TAX CUTS AND SOCIAL PROGRAMMES

The tax cuts and social programmes during the Bush, Obama and Trump administrations, coupled with increased military spending, significantly strained U.S. finances. Under George W. Bush, tax cuts, especially on income and estate taxes, reduced federal revenues by approximately USD 1.5 trillion over ten years. These cuts were intended to stimulate economic growth but contributed heavily to rising deficits. Between 2001 and 2009, U.S. expenditures on the Iraq and Afghanistan wars amounted to around USD 1.9 trillion, exacerbating the nation's fiscal imbalance.

Barack Obama, responding to the Great Recession, enacted a USD 787 billion stimulus package through the American Recovery and Reinvestment Act (ARRA) of 2009. [1] While it helped revive the economy, it also increased the federal deficit, which surged to USD 1.4 trillion, the highest since World War II. Obama's administration also passed the Dodd-Frank Act [2] to regulate financial firms post-GFC, further adding to government spending.

Donald Trump's Tax Cuts and Jobs Act (TCJA) of 2017 [3] reduced corporate tax rates from 35% to 21% and lowered income taxes for individuals. Despite claims of stimulating the economy, the TCJA contributed to growing deficits, with the national deficit reaching USD 779 billion in 2018 and surpassing USD 1 trillion in 2019.

Joe Biden's early presidency saw the introduction of the American Rescue Plan (ARP) in 2021 [4], a USD 1.9 trillion relief package aimed at COVID-19 recovery. The package extended unemployment benefits, funded vaccine distribution and expanded the child tax credit, driving the federal deficit to USD 3.1 trillion in 2020, the largest in U.S. history. The deficit remained high at USD 2.8 trillion in 2021, adding substantially to the national debt.

FED'S UNCONVENTIONAL MONETARY POLICIES

Although inflation remained subdued for much of the 2010s, the post-pandemic era saw a sharp resurgence. By 2022 and 2023, inflation surged to its highest levels in decades, prompting the Fed to raise interest rates aggressively. This raised doubts about the Fed's ability to manage inflation effectively, further destabilising confidence in the USD as a stable reserve currency.

GLOBAL TREMORS

EUR AS A CHALLENGER TO THE USD'S DOMINANCE

The EUR was introduced on January 1, 1999, with high hopes of becoming a viable alternative to the USD as the world's reserve currency. However, soon after its launch, the eurozone faced economic slowdowns and the EUR traded below parity against the USD. The U.K.'s decision to leave the EU under Brexit further weakened the EUR's position. Despite these challenges, the EUR has regained strength against the USD post-COVID-19.

The EUR faces its own set of challenges in competing with the USD. The European Union (EU) consists of diverse economies at varying stages of economic development, making it difficult for the European Central Bank (ECB) to implement unified monetary policies. The lack of fiscal harmonisation among EU member states complicates the enforcement of fiscal discipline, as individual countries prioritise domestic fiscal policies over EU-wide agreements. The absence of full fiscal integration within the EU remains a significant challenge for the EUR's potential to rival the USD.

RMB AS AN EMERGING CANDIDATE

The rise of China as a global economic power and its efforts to internationalise the RMB have made it a credible challenger to the USD. China's Belt and Road Initiative (BRI) has expanded its economic influence across Asia, Africa and Europe, encouraging the use of the RMB in trade agreements and infrastructure projects. This initiative has gradually increased the RMB's role in international finance, though it remains far from surpassing the USD's global dominance.

China has signed multiple bilateral agreements to settle trade in RMB, bypassing the USD. In energy trade with Russia, for example, some transactions are conducted in RMB. In 2016, the International Monetary Fund (IMF) included the RMB in its basket of Special Drawing Rights (SDRs), a milestone marking China's growing financial influence.

For the RMB to challenge the USD more effectively, China must focus on three key areas:

Political Clout: China's foreign policy needs to be strategically articulated, strengthening ties with regional neighbours and non-aligned countries. A clear and coherent diplomatic strategy will enhance trust in China's commitment to fostering economic relations.

Economic Clout: The success of China's BRI is an important aspect of its economic influence. While some BRI projects have encountered difficulties, countries such as Cambodia and Indonesia have benefited greatly from Chinese investment and infrastructure development.

Belt and Road Initiatives
Expressway from Phnom Penh to Sihanoukville: shortening travelling time between these two cities from 4 hours to 2 hours. Constructed under BRI and under a Build Operate Transfer (BOT) for about 50 years
Funan Techo Canal: a waterway linking Phnom Penh to seaport Kampot now under construction. This waterway will shorten logistical routes and save on tariffs paid to Vietnam for using Vietnamese waterways. Partially funded by Chinese Government under BRI with BOT agreement for about 50 years
Whoosh: Chinese gave substantial financing for the construction of a high-speed rail service between Jakarta and Bandung, Indonesia. The travel time was reduced from 3 hours to 45 minutes.

Financial Infrastructure: For the RMB to be more widely adopted, China must continue to develop its financial systems and markets, ensuring they are open, transparent and trusted by international investors and trade partners.

China's efforts in these areas, combined with its growing economic influence, position the RMB as a serious contender to the USD, though its global dominance is still distant.

In addition to the Belt and Road Initiative (BRI), China must focus on expanding its middle-class consumer base, which plays a crucial role in shifting the economy from its traditional reliance on exports toward more robust domestic consumption. Strengthening the consumer sector is vital for driving GDP growth, as a larger middle class increases domestic demand, supporting overall economic expansion. This will also enhance the circulation of the RMB within the domestic economy, creating the foundation for the RMB's further integration into international trade. A more widespread use of the RMB in global transactions will strengthen its case as a potential reserve currency.

Furthermore, China must continue to enhance its **Policy Clout**. This includes the gradual relaxation of currency controls, moving towards a more market-determined and freer-floating currency. The People's Bank of China (PBOC) must implement clear, credible and transparent monetary policies that encourage trust and predictability in the RMB. Along with market-oriented reforms, a consistent and well-communicated policy approach regarding business, trade and international relations will help China build credibility on the global stage. By aligning its actions with clearly defined policies and acting with consistency, China can elevate its reputation and stature within the international community, which is crucial for the RMB to gain traction as a preferred global currency.

A Ten Chinese Yuan note issued by Bank of China in 1937 showing Dr Sun Yat-Sen, Father of the Chinese Republic

A Five Chinese Yuan note likely issued by the Central Bank of China in 1930

BLOCKCHAIN, DIGITAL AND CRYPTO CURRENCIES

The rise of blockchain technology and digital currencies is reshaping the global financial landscape, potentially challenging the dominance of the U.S. dollar (USD) in the long run. The introduction of government-backed Central Bank Digital Currencies (CBDCs), such as China's Digital Yuan and exploratory projects in the European Union and Japan, signifies a growing shift toward digital solutions in trade and finance. These initiatives may alter the global balance if they outpace the U.S. in development and adoption. Meanwhile, decentralised cryptocurrencies like Bitcoin and Ethereum have sparked discussions about the future of money, though their current role in international trade and finance remains limited due to inherent challenges such as cybersecurity and cross-border legal issues.

Challenges with Cryptocurrencies

Cryptocurrencies, despite their innovative appeal, face significant hurdles. Their high price volatility complicates their use as a medium of exchange in trade, as unpredictable fluctuations make pricing and forecasting difficult. Furthermore, the decentralised and largely unregulated nature of cryptocurrencies exposes them to fraud, cyber-theft and misuse. Events like the FTX collapse and controversies surrounding Binance have underscored these vulnerabilities, raising doubts about the reliability of cryptocurrencies for large-scale economic activities.

For cryptocurrencies to become viable alternatives in international trade, they will need to address critical issues like price stability, security and regulatory oversight. Without these, their potential to challenge traditional fiat currencies, including the USD, remains uncertain.

Blockchain: Beyond Cryptocurrencies

At its core, blockchain is a decentralised electronic ledger system that securely records transactions across a network of computers (nodes). This decentralised approach ensures transparency, security and resistance to tampering. Blockchain technology has already demonstrated its value in areas such as supply chain management, digital identity verification and secure financial transactions.

The distinction between blockchain as a technology and the cryptocurrencies built upon it is crucial. While cryptocurrencies face volatility and regulatory challenges, blockchain itself is increasingly being adopted by financial institutions and governments. Many are exploring blockchain-based systems for processing traditional fiat currency transactions, including the development of CBDCs. These blockchain applications promise faster, more secure and transparent financial systems.

Implications for the USD

The advent of CBDCs and blockchain-based systems could gradually erode the USD's dominance in international trade and finance if other nations outpace the U.S. in adoption. However, the USD's entrenched position as the world's reserve currency and the scale of the U.S. financial system provide a strong counterbalance.

Blockchain technology, meanwhile, offers opportunities to modernise financial systems globally, fostering efficiency and transparency. Its impact may not only complement but also transform traditional currency systems, demonstrating that its potential extends far beyond cryptocurrencies.

Illustration: *A buyer converts fiat currency to cryptocurrency on the blockchain platform and transfers to the Seller. The Seller converts the cryptocurrency to another fiat currency of Seller's choice on the same platform and onward transfers the received fiat currency to another payment platform. CBDCs are structured similar to such blockchain framework.*

In conclusion, while blockchain and digital currencies are disrupting traditional finance, their ability to significantly alter the global economic order depends on resolving key challenges and achieving widespread adoption. The USD's position may face growing competition, but its immediate displacement remains uncertain.

ALTERNATIVE PAYMENT PLATFORMS

The SWIFT system has long been the backbone of global USD-denominated transactions, ensuring efficient clearing and settlement. However, for any currency to challenge the USD's dominance, there must be alternative payment and settlement platforms for other currencies. As technology advances in the financial sector, new payment systems are emerging to facilitate trade settlements in currencies beyond the USD, particularly in the consumer and e-commerce sectors.

One such platform is China's Cross-Border Payment System (CIPS), which was introduced in 2015 to enable RMB trade settlements. The RMB has grown to become the third-largest trade finance currency and the fifth-largest payment currency in recent years, according to the IMF. It is part of the Special Drawing Rights (SDR) basket of the International Monetary Fund. The CIPS system, which has been widely adopted in 103 countries, including Japan, Russia and Brazil, has gained traction as an alternative international payment system for the RMB. Notably, U.S. sanctions on Russia following the Russia-Ukraine war pushed Russia to engage in oil trade with China via CIPS, bypassing traditional USD-based systems.

Additionally, numerous fintech payment platforms, such as AirWallex, Stripe and PayPal, are offering innovative solutions that use open or closed APIs (Application Programming Interfaces) to facilitate electronic transfers of funds between counterparties. These platforms provide flexibility and alternative payment routes outside the traditional banking systems. Furthermore, regional digital payment solutions like Cambodia's Bakong System (based on blockchain technology) and Singapore's PayNow System, which is integrating with Malaysia's payment platforms, further contribute to the diversification of cross-border payment systems.

Though these fintech platforms act as intermediaries between national clearing systems and end-users, the technology behind them has the potential to be scaled into national solutions, thereby laying the groundwork for more global alternatives to the USD-dominated financial infrastructure. As these alternatives develop, they pose a challenge to the USD's dominance in global trade and finance. [Study Notes 5]

SEISMIC SHIFTS

While SWIFT remains the dominant method for cross-border payments conducted in USD, alternatives are emerging and gaining traction. With increasing numbers of countries and businesses opting for trade agreements that bypass U.S. involvement, the landscape of international payments is evolving. These alternatives, such as China's CIPS system for RMB settlements and various fintech platforms like AirWallex and PayPal, offer new options for secure and efficient transactions.

As more trading blocs and nations explore non-USD payment systems, businesses will have a wider array of platforms to choose from, reducing reliance on the U.S. dollar. This shift marks the beginning of a period of experimentation and adjustment, as countries and companies test and refine these alternatives. While SWIFT still holds the lead, the growing availability and adoption of alternative payment and settlement systems signal a change in the global financial infrastructure. The coming years will likely see a gradual diversification in payment systems as countries seek to mitigate risks associated with reliance on U.S.-dominated platforms.

BLACK SWAN EVENT - COVID-19 PANDEMIC

COVID-19 was a major shock to the global system, a "black swan" event of extreme magnitude. The pandemic led to millions of deaths and a massive economic response, particularly from the U.S. government. Trillions of dollars were spent on stimulus packages, direct payments to individuals, unemployment benefits and business aid, all funded by borrowing. This unprecedented spending pushed U.S. national debt to new heights, raising concerns about the long-term sustainability of U.S. fiscal policy and the value of the U.S. dollar.

The Federal Reserve's interventions also escalated, with massive asset purchases through Quantitative Easing and other emergency measures. While these actions provided short-term economic relief, they fuelled fears about inflation and currency devaluation. By 2021-2023, inflation surged to levels not seen in decades, further eroding confidence in the dollar's stability.

The USD's dominance was already facing challenges before the pandemic, including the Global Financial Crisis, military conflicts, the rise of China and growing efforts to bypass the dollar in international trade. The introduction of the EUR and the rise of the

RMB as a global trade currency, along with the growing interest in digital currencies, added new layers of competition for the dollar's role as the world's reserve currency.

Despite these mounting concerns, the USD continues to hold its position as the primary global reserve currency due to the deep liquidity of U.S. financial markets and the trust placed in U.S. institutions. However, the convergence of geopolitical, economic and financial shifts suggests that the status quo is increasingly unsustainable in the long term. The rise of alternative currencies and payment systems, coupled with the U.S.'s mounting debt and inflationary pressures, signals that the USD's dominance could eventually be challenged. The world is on the cusp of potentially significant changes in the global monetary landscape.

CONTINUED AUDACITY OF USD

The current global situation reveals the immense challenges faced by countries holding U.S. Treasuries (USTs) and underscores the tension between the U.S.'s debt trajectory and its continued dominance of the global financial system. The U.S. can issue bonds and the world continues to purchase them for several reasons, despite growing concerns about the sustainability of the USD and the U.S. economy.

THE ILLOGIC OF U.S. BOND BUYERS

Countries that hold USTs are, in essence, lending money to the U.S. government. This raises a critical question:

Why would nations continue to purchase these bonds when the U.S. faces mounting debt, political instability and an uncertain economic future?
The answer is the lack of attractive alternatives.

Many of these countries earn USD through trade with the U.S. (i.e., exports). While they may not trust the long-term stability of the USD, they have few viable options to invest their USD earnings. Converting all their USD into physical gold or other non-USD assets is not ideal because gold doesn't offer interest, and many countries simply lack the financial infrastructure to make large-scale non-USD investments. Thus, they continue purchasing USTs, despite the inherent risks.

This situation reflects the classic dilemma: even if one doesn't trust the USD in the long term, the lack of better options means they have little choice but to keep holding U.S. debt. The USD still serves as the global benchmark currency and most international trade is conducted in USD, which means countries must hold it to participate in global commerce. The alternative is to face potential liquidity issues or trade constraints.

The *"sinking ship"* metaphor captures the growing anxiety. If the political and economic instability in the U.S. continues, many countries may eventually be forced to reconsider their reliance on U.S. debt. If countries continue to pile on more U.S. debt to their reserve portfolio, it is like *"laying out more deck chairs on a sinking ship"*, not a prudent decision to make. On the other hand, finding a viable alternative for global reserves and investment remains a monumental challenge.

THE PRIVILEGE OF BEING A RESERVE CURRENCY

One of the central privileges of the USD is its status as the world's reserve currency. The U.S. benefits from the ability to print money, with the cost of producing a USD100 bill far less than its face value. This allows the U.S. to run trade deficits and finance massive debt, as the rest of the world is willing to hold USD-denominated assets. This "magic" enables the U.S. to enjoy unparalleled economic flexibility, particularly when financing its government debt through bond issuance.

But this privilege is not guaranteed forever. History shows that dominant global currencies eventually lose their supremacy, as in the cases of the British pound during the decline of the British Empire and the Japanese yen post-World War II. Countries and investors are increasingly aware of the risks to the USD's long-term dominance and the rise of alternative currencies (like the EUR, the Chinese RMB, and digital currencies) further highlights the potential for a shift in the global financial system.

THE ELEPHANT IN THE ROOM

Years ago, my book editor-friend visited Kruger National Park in South Africa and embarked on an elephant safari. During the journey, the guide shared an insightful observation: due to its sheer size and strength, the elephant has no natural predators. However, the guide also pointed out that the most significant threats to elephants are human-induced: poaching, habitat destruction and human-elephant conflicts. These challenges, created by human activities, pose far greater dangers to the survival of elephants than any natural predator ever could.

The analogy of the *"Elephant in the Room"* serves as a compelling reflection of the USD's status as the world's reserve currency now facing *a massive pile of U.S. debt and the global dependency on USD-denominated assets*. Much like the majestic elephant, the USD currently has no natural rivals capable of displacing it. Its dominance in global trade, financial markets and reserve holdings mirrors the elephant's unrivalled stature in the wild. However, just as the elephant faces its greatest threats not from predators but from human actions; poaching, habitat loss and conflict, the USD's vulnerabilities stem from human-driven issues: quantitative easing (QE), excessive government spending and uncontrolled money printing. These actions erode trust in the currency's value and stability over time.

In both the wild and the financial ecosystem, human behaviours hold the key to survival or decline. For the elephant, it is conservation and coexistence; for the USD, it is fiscal discipline and prudent policymaking. The parallels remind us that even the most dominant entities can be brought low by neglect or mismanagement, underscoring the need for vigilance and responsibility to avoid tipping points.

For now, countries face a difficult balancing act: they are hesitant to drastically reduce their holdings of U.S. debt for fear of disrupting the global financial system, but the growing risks associated with the USD mean that alternatives may eventually become more attractive. The process of diversifying away from the USD will likely be slow, but as the U.S.'s economic and political challenges continue, the foundations of the USD's dominance will likely be increasingly questioned.

In conclusion, the privileged status of the USD as the world's reserve currency allows the U.S. to print money and finance its massive debt without the same immediate consequences that other nations would face. However, with growing concerns about the sustainability of U.S. debt, the long-term value of the USD and the emergence of alternative currencies, the global financial system is entering a period of uncertainty. How countries will navigate this uncertainty and whether any currency will emerge to rival the U.S. Dollar remains to be seen. The status quo may not be sustainable forever, and the world may soon face a transition to a new global reserve currency system.

In the book written by Barry Eichengreen, **"EXHORBITANT PRIVILEGE"** (Suggested Reading List [2], page 4), Charles de Gaulle's finance minister, Valéry Giscard d'Estaing, referred to America's **"exorbitant privilege"**. This **"privilege"** was and still is a sore point for foreigners being subjected to an asymmetric financial system such that USD, being the world's reserve currency, qualified and still qualifies the U.S. government to borrow eye-popping amounts from the world at relatively lower interest rates despite its deteriorating fiscal conditions and declining terms of trade.

VISIBILITY OF CRACKS

It appears that the process of diversifying away from USD has happened but evidently at a gradual pace. (Figure5a).

World Aggregated Currency Composition of Official Foreign Exchange Reserves									
	2016	2017	2018	2019	2020	2021	2022	2023	2024
Shares of Allocated Reserves	78.52	87.43	93.82	93.64	93.40	93.23	92.64	92.76	92.86
% holdings of USD	65.36	62.73	61.76	60.75	58.92	58.80	58.52	58.42	58.22
% holdings of EUR	19.14	20.17	20.67	20.59	21.29	20.59	20.37	19.94	19.76
% holdings of RMB	1.08	1.23	1.89	1.94	2.29	2.80	2.61	2.29	2.14
% holdings of JPY	3.95	4.90	5.19	5.87	6.03	5.52	5.54	5.69	5.59
% holdings of GBP	4.35	4.54	4.43	4.64	4.73	4.81	4.90	4.86	4.94
% holdings of AUD, Aussie $	1.69	1.80	1.63	1.70	1.83	1.84	1.97	2.14	2.24
% holdings of CAD, Canadian $	1.94	2.03	1.84	1.86	2.08	2.38	2.39	2.59	2.68
% holdings of CHF, Swiss Francs	0.16	0.18	0.14	0.15	0.17	0.17	0.23	0.19	0.20
% holdings of Other Currencies	2.33	2.43	2.45	2.51	2.65	3.09	3.48	3.87	4.25
% holdings of Unallocated Reserves	21.48	12.57	6.18	6.36	6.60	6.77	7.36	7.24	7.14
Source: Currency Composition of Official Foreign Exchange Reserves (COFER). International Financial Statistics (IFS)									
Data extracted from http://data.imf.org/ on: 11/9/2024 11:42:27 PM									

Figure 5a: *World's Aggregated Composition of Official Foreign Exchange Reserves. The trend is showing that USD composition if trending lower whilst RMB is gradually increasing. Individual countries' composition is usually confidential and difficult to obtain.*

In the global trading market share, USD is still the dominant currency of trade. The use of RMB in international transactions is also showing some utility momentum with RMB's market share being 1.1% of world transactions in 2013 and up to 2.5% in May 2023. According to a Goldman Sachs economist, Maggie Wei who wrote in her team report in July 2023 [5], RMB's use in payments worldwide is still limited. However, this trade measure increased to 3.61% in September 2024. Slowly but surely, we are seeing cracks in USD's role as a trading currency becoming visible. (Figure 5b)

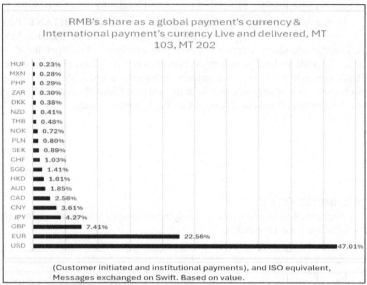

Figure 5b: *Percentage of trade volumes of currencies as of September 2024, indicating USD's dominance with EUR coming in 2nd, GBP 3rd, JPY 4th and RMB in 5th position. However, RMB's market share has increased. Information extracted from SWIFT.*

HISTORY REPEATING ITSELF

Throughout history, major global currencies like the British Pound (GBP) and the U.S. Dollar (USD) have faced dramatic single-step devaluations, driven by economic crises, systemic pressures or deliberate policy decisions.

In **1931**, Britain abandoned the gold standard, devaluing the GBP by approximately **25%** to combat a severe economic downturn and restore export competitiveness.

The **Sterling Crisis** and the associated devaluation of the British Pound by **14.3%** occurred on **November 18, 1967**, under the government of Prime Minister Harold Wilson. The crisis was triggered by mounting economic pressures, including a significant trade deficit, declining confidence in the UK's economy and speculative attacks on the pound. The UK government eventually abandoned efforts to defend the pound's value, devaluing it from **$2.80 to $2.40**, marking a major single-step devaluation.

The USD has also seen significant realignments. In **1971**, the collapse of the Bretton Woods System marked the end of the dollar's fixed link to gold, effectively devaluing the USD as it transitioned to a fiat currency system.

Another pivotal moment came with the **Plaza Accord of 1985**, where the U.S. and four other major economies agreed to a coordinated devaluation of the USD. This policy-driven adjustment, aimed at addressing trade imbalances, led to a steep decline in the USD's value, nearly **50% against the JPY** over two years.

These episodes reveal the recurring nature of dramatic currency shifts in response to economic realities, echoing Karl Marx's reflection that *"history repeats itself, first as tragedy, then as farce."* Whether through crises-driven necessity or calculated policy, such devaluations highlight the cyclical challenges faced by even the world's most dominant currencies.

MISGUIDED SCEPTICISM
The factors mentioned in the **"Continued Audacity USD"** section earlier could have led many market participants to be sceptical about any USD devaluation soon. The long-term risks appear to have been ignored.

Erosion of Confidence: Persistent twin deficits and political gridlock could erode trust in the USD, especially if fiscal discipline is not restored.

Emerging Alternatives: Over time, initiatives like BRICS currencies or digital currencies could challenge the USD's dominance.

Inflationary Pressures: Excessive money printing to finance deficits can weaken the USD, as seen during episodes like the 1970s inflation crisis.

While outright scepticism about immediate devaluation is understandable, history suggests that prolonged fiscal mismanagement can eventually lead to currency adjustments, whether gradual or abrupt. As global dynamics evolve, the factors shielding the USD today may weaken, bringing the risks of devaluation back into focus.

Chapter 6
Bracing and Preparing for the Demise
How we should prepare ourselves as individuals, financial institutions, sovereign nations? The scenarios that could unfold should the demise of the USD happen and Wishful Thinking for an ideal reserve currency.

The tale of the USD echoes Edmond Dantès's journey in *The Count of Monte Cristo*, a story of dominance, privilege and the threat of eventual reckoning. For decades, the USD has reigned as the world's reserve currency, bolstered by trust, liquidity and the strength of U.S. financial markets. But just as Dantès's betrayers; Danglars, Mondego and de Villefort succumbed to their flaws, the USD faces rising threats.

Rivals on the Rise
The EUR and the RMB are challenging the USD's supremacy. Like Mondego's envy, their ambition is fuelled by opportunities to displace the dominant force. Mondego, driven by personal jealousy and insecurity, sought power through deceit, just as these rival currencies are striving to undercut the USD's position. The EUR's resilience post-COVID-19 and the RMB's rise through economic growth and China's Belt and Road Initiative have laid the groundwork. Yet, both face hurdles: the EUR struggles with EU fragmentation, while the RMB remains shackled by currency controls. Their rise is slow, but the cracks in the USD's armour are showing.

The Greed of Borrowing
The U.S. government's unchecked spending mirrors Danglars's insatiable greed. Danglars, a character consumed by financial ambition, betrayed Edmond for wealth, much like how excessive borrowing, stimulus packages and tax cuts have inflated U.S. debt levels, slowly eroding confidence in the USD. Nations holding U.S. Treasuries have limited alternatives for their USD earnings, trapped between the risk of holding USD and the instability of other assets. Yet history reminds us that no currency, not even the British Pound Sterling, is invincible.

The Illusion of Stability
De Villefort's ambition, masked by a veneer of respectability, led to his undoing, just as the U.S.'s overreach in fiscal and foreign policy threatens the USD. De Villefort, driven by political ambition and moral compromise, manipulated the system for personal gain, ultimately exposing the flaws of his own machinations. Political tremors, from wars to sanctions, have shaken faith in the USD, while inflation and growing debt cast shadows over its future. The USD's privilege as a reserve currency, where the cost of printing a USD100 note is far less than its value, feels increasingly precarious. As Edmond's fiancée, Mercédès, watches him transform into the vengeful Count, nations may soon witness the USD's transformation from a symbol of power to a harbinger of decline. Mercédès, who remained devoted to Edmond despite years of loss, symbolises the emotional and personal cost of prolonged dominance and the eventual, inevitable change.

Waiting and Hoping
As Dantès left us with the words "Wait and Hope," so too does the world wait to see if the USD will falter. The transition, should it come, will be chaotic. Four signs would mark its decline: **reduced use in global trade** *(dropping from 50% to 25%)*, **eroding reserve status** *(less than 25% of cumulative central banks' reserve portfolio)*, **diminished**

role in commodity pricing (death of the Petrodollar) **and a weakening U.S. economy** *(sustained sub-par GDP growth, below 1%).*

The USD remains the Count of currencies, but the tides of history are unrelenting. To avoid being caught in the wreckage, nations, institutions and individuals must prepare for a world where the USD's dominance may no longer be assured.

INDIVIDUALS

The tale of USD's potential decline carries a profound lesson for individuals and families. As history has shown, a single reliance on fiat currencies, much like the "Banana Notes" during World War II, can lead to financial ruin when those currencies collapse. Diversification of wealth is not just prudent; it is essential for survival in times of crisis. Take the example of the 1997 Asian Financial Crisis. Indonesian families, valuing education, sent their children abroad, often to Singapore. But when the Indonesian Rupiah (IDR) devalued sixfold from IDR2,500 to IDR15,000 against the USD, many found themselves unable to sustain their children's overseas education. Businesses faltered, liquidity dried up and financial plans crumbled. This crisis demonstrated how an overreliance on one currency could upend lives.

The lesson? ***Diversification.*** A diversified currency portfolio can help cushion against external shocks. Physical assets such as real estate, gold and silver offer stability and utility. Real estate provides shelter and productive uses, while gold and silver, accepted for millennia as stores of value, transcend geopolitical and economic turmoil. Even during transitions of power and crises, such as the decimation of the Banana Dollar during the Japanese occupation, gold retained its intrinsic value, becoming a lifeline for those who had it.

THE VALUE OF PHYSICAL ASSETS: LESSONS FROM HISTORY

During WWII, the Japanese Banana Dollar went from being equivalent to the Malayan Dollar at the start of the occupation to worthless by the end, losing 950 times its value. Those who depended solely on these notes saw their wealth crumble Conversely, those holding gold or silver could trade them for essentials, as these metals retained their purchasing power. This enduring value is why central banks hoard gold reserves and why even fictional villains, as in *Die Hard with a Vengeance,* sought to steal the gold bullion from the Federal Reserve Bank of New York. If the bad guys understood the value of gold, shouldn't we?

PRACTICAL STEPS FOR INDIVIDUALS

To navigate a world where USD dominance may wane, individuals should:

Diversify Portfolios: Avoid heavy reliance on any single currency. Incorporate assets denominated in multiple currencies and invest in real estate and commodities.

Hold Physical Gold and Silver: These timeless assets are universally recognised and serve as a hedge against inflation and currency devaluation.

Stay Informed: Monitor geopolitical and economic developments that might impact currencies and investments.

Develop Risk Management Plans: Be prepared for financial shocks by minimising concentration risks and maintaining liquidity.

Invest Prudently: Opt for controlled, calculated risks over speculation, ensuring a stable foundation for financial security.

The lesson from crises past is clear: wealth tied to transient fiat currencies can vanish overnight, but physical assets endure. Like Edmond Dantès preparing for his revenge, individuals must be deliberate, resourceful and forward-thinking, ensuring they are ready when the tremors of financial upheaval strike.

BE LEARNED, BE INFORMED

The world of investments offers an overwhelming array of options, from diverse products to professional advisory services. Yet, amidst this abundance, one truth remains: ***the ultimate responsibility for financial outcomes lies with the individual***. Gains, losses, prudence and greed all originate and conclude with personal decisions.

To navigate this complex landscape, one must continuously seek knowledge and remain informed. Markets shift, strategies evolve and new opportunities arise, demanding our vigilance and wisdom to act when necessary. The best hedge is not merely financial; it is intellectual, rooted in learning, critical thinking and proactive decision-making.

This journey is not prescriptive but empowering. It is a call to action, urging individuals to investigate, learn and build the understanding needed to ***"prepare and act"*** rather than passively ***"wait and hope"***.

Benjamin Franklin, whose visage graces the U.S. One Hundred Dollar Note, encapsulates this philosophy perfectly:

"If a man empties his purse into his head, no man can take it away from him. An investment in knowledge always pays the best dividends."

Let this wisdom guide us in charting our paths through the uncertainties of the financial world.

FINANCIAL INSTITUTIONs AND INVESTMENT FIRMs (FIIFs)

For ***Financial Institutions and Investment Firms (FIIFs)***, managing risk exposure and maintaining readiness are paramount. Like individuals, FIIFs must be vigilant in looking out for and anticipating unforeseen financial shocks, especially the so-called "black swan" events—rare and unpredictable occurrences with significant consequences. While the timing or nature of such events cannot be foreseen, their potential fallout can be appraised and mitigated.

FIIFs must construct and maintain resilient portfolios capable of withstanding these tremors. This involves robust risk monitoring and management systems, proactive stress-testing and strategies to minimise damage. History has shown that leverage and liquidity are the two main vulnerabilities that exacerbate portfolio fragility during crises:

Leverage: Excessive borrowing amplifies gains in good times but magnifies losses in downturns. Reducing overexposure and maintaining prudent debt levels are crucial to safeguarding stability.

Liquidity: In times of distress, illiquid assets can trap institutions, leaving them unable to meet obligations or respond to market shocks. Ensuring a balanced mix of liquid and illiquid assets, along with contingency plans, is critical.

Resilience is built not just on risk aversion but on readiness by creating structures and strategies that ensure survival and position for recovery when the storm subsides. (see Chapter 3 [Box 3A] for Leverage explanation)

LEVERAGE AND LIQUIDITY: A DOUBLE-EDGED SWORD

The intertwined issues of leverage and liquidity have been recurring culprits in financial crises, as illustrated by notable collapses across different geographies and eras. While leverage offers the allure of amplified returns, it equally magnifies risks, especially when combined with liquidity constraints.

The 1997 Financial Crisis and Korea's Chaebols

During the Asian Financial Crisis, Korea's *chaebols*, large family-owned conglomerates, found themselves precariously exposed. Many had borrowed excessively, often in USD, to finance their ambitious growth. When the crisis unfolded, liquidity evaporated, exchange rates soared and servicing USD-denominated debt became untenable. Unable to repay or refinance their obligations, several *chaebols* faced collapse. The Korean government, with assistance from the International Monetary Fund (IMF), had to step in to prevent further economic disintegration. This episode highlighted how excessive leverage, especially in foreign currency, becomes a liability in times of financial distress. [1]

Long-Term Capital Management (LTCM): A Lesson in Overreach

Around the same time, U.S.-based hedge fund Long-Term Capital Management (LTCM) made highly leveraged bets on arbitraging *(an attempt to capture price anomalies of assets trading in different markets)* fixed-income securities. When Russia defaulted on its non-Ruble debt in 1998, LTCM's portfolio suffered catastrophic losses. With collateral calls and no liquidity to unwind its positions, LTCM teetered on the brink of collapse. Recognising the systemic risk posed by LTCM's interconnectedness, the Federal Reserve orchestrated a bailout involving several major financial institutions. The firm's downfall underscored the danger of overleveraged positions meeting illiquid markets, a potent cocktail for financial disaster. [2]

Lehman Brothers: Leverage's Final Blow

The 2008 financial crisis saw another dramatic example of leverage's destructive power in the example of Lehman Brothers. With USD 600 billion in assets backed by only USD 20 billion in liquid reserves, Lehman operated with a staggering 30:1 leverage ratio. [3] A mere 3.33% decline in asset value was enough to obliterate its equity cushion, and the subprime mortgage meltdown did just that. Unlike LTCM, there was no lifeline for Lehman and its bankruptcy sent shockwaves through global markets. Lehman's collapse mirrored the avarice of Danglars in *The Count of Monte Cristo*, a fall driven by unchecked greed and overconfidence.

Lessons Learned

Across these cases, the combination of leverage and liquidity, or rather, their mismanagement, proved fatal. While leverage can accelerate growth, its risks are amplified in crises, particularly when liquidity dries up. Whether in Korea's *chaebols*, LTCM or Lehman Brothers, the lessons are clear: prudent leverage limits, diversified funding and maintaining sufficient liquidity buffers are indispensable for long-term stability. Like the tragic flaws of Monte Cristo's adversaries, the greed and overreach that fuel leverage often lead to a self-inflicted downfall.

DURATION MANAGEMENT: NAVIGATING FIXED INCOME RISKS

Duration management is a cornerstone of fixed-income portfolio strategy, vital for navigating interest rate risks. At its core, this practice involves balancing bond maturities to optimise returns in fluctuating interest rate environments. Overweighting long-dated bonds in a declining interest rate climate and underweighting them when rates are rising is Duration Management 101. However, managing bond portfolios often transcends these basics, requiring nuanced approaches to maturity structures and credit profiles.

Silicon Valley Bank (SVB): A Failure in Duration Management

Silicon Valley Bank, with assets exceeding USD 200 billion at its peak, became a cautionary tale of mismanaging interest rate risk. SVB invested heavily in long-dated U.S. Treasuries while relying on short-term deposits for funding. When the Federal Reserve implemented rapid interest rate hikes, the market value of these long-dated bonds plummeted. SVB found itself unable to meet deposit withdrawals as its bond holdings were worth less than its liabilities. Attempts to raise equity capital failed, triggering a bank run and eventual collapse. SVB's management later admitted to neglecting proper hedging strategies for its interest rate exposure, a critical lapse in duration management. [4]

Norinchukin Bank (Norchu): A Miscalculation of Rates

In June 2024, Japan's Norinchukin Bank announced a staggering USD 9.5 billion loss on its overseas fixed-income portfolio. Similar to SVB, Norchu's unhedged exposure to long-dated U.S. fixed-income securities left it vulnerable to unexpected spikes in U.S. interest rates. Unlike SVB, Norchu appeared to make an explicit albeit erroneous bet that long-term U.S. interest rates would remain stable. The lack of hedging compounded the impact of this miscalculation. [5]

The Bigger Picture: Asset-Liability Management (ALM) and Systemic Risks

Asset-Liability Management (ALM) is a discipline that financial institutions and investment firms (FIIFs) typically prioritise, making the oversights at SVB and Norchu glaring anomalies. However, the broader concern lies in the herd mentality within financial markets. When numerous institutions chase the same asset class, whether it be a specific bond duration in fixed income or a hot sector in equities, risk concentration rises exponentially. This collective behaviour can lead to systemic vulnerabilities where the failure of a few players has ripple effects throughout the global financial system, potentially triggering another Global Financial Crisis (GFC).

LESSONS FOR RESILIENCE

Hedging Is Non-Negotiable: As seen in SVB and Norchu's cases, unhedged positions amplify risks. Effective duration management requires robust hedging strategies to offset potential losses.

Scenario Analysis and Stress Testing: Regularly modelling "what-if" scenarios for interest rate shocks can prepare institutions for unexpected market movements.

Diversification and Risk Monitoring: Avoiding excessive exposure to specific durations, asset classes or sectors mitigates systemic risk.

Prudent ALM Practices: A mismatch between assets and liabilities, as seen in SVB's reliance on short-term deposits, is a fundamental flaw that can erode institutional stability.

Much like the interconnectedness of Danglars' greed, Villefort's ambition and Mondego's envy in *The Count of Monte Cristo*, financial crises often arise from intertwined vulnerabilities. Each oversight in managing duration or liquidity adds to the fragility of the system, and without corrective action, the consequences can be catastrophic. The SVB and Norchu episodes serve as stark reminders of the necessity for vigilance and discipline in navigating the ever-evolving dynamics of financial markets.

RISK MANAGEMENT OF EXTREMITIES

Long-Term Capital Management (LTCM), despite employing Nobel laureates and sophisticated mathematical models, unravelled under the weight of unforeseen extremities. Their failure stemmed from assumptions that crumbled during a black swan event. In times of extreme market distress, liquidity dries up, bid-offer spreads *(buy-sell price gaps)* widen dramatically and asset valuations nosedive. These rapid developments can decimate cash collateral, particularly in highly leveraged setups. This cascade of events has been a hallmark of financial crises past and likely for those yet to come.

Flaws in Current Risk Management Approaches

Risk management frameworks at most Financial Institutions and Investment Firms (FIIFs) focus on how portfolios react under predefined market scenarios. Stop-loss thresholds, derived from these scenarios, serve as a safeguard. However, such strategies, often grounded in quantitative methodologies, may overlook critical qualitative factors:

Lack of Exit Options: *Markets may seize, offering no viable price for trade exits.*
Unexpected Loss Magnitudes: *Even unleveraged positions can spiral into severe losses.*
Irrational Behaviour: *Panic-driven market participants amplify volatility.*
Fragile Institutions: *Respected entities or frameworks can collapse under duress.*

These gaps highlight the need for more comprehensive strategies that address not just anticipated risks but also the extremities of unexpected market behaviour.

THE CASE FOR EXTREME RISK MITIGATION (ERM)

Unlike traditional risk management, Extreme Risk Mitigation (ERM) is about preparing for the unthinkable. It blends statistical and quantitative tools with insights from diverse disciplines like behavioural science, financial history and international law. ERM shifts the focus from prevention (risk management) to response (damage control). For example:

Risk Management: *Implementing safeguards to prevent milk from spilling.*
Risk Mitigation: *Preparing to contain and clean up spilled milk when it inevitably occurs.*

This nuanced approach can make the difference between resilience and collapse when crises strike.

LESSONS FOR FIIFS AND USD PREPAREDNESS

Despite their sophistication, many FIIFs lack robust ERM frameworks tailored to seismic global events like the potential decline of the USD as the world's reserve currency. Developing a practical ERM plan is often deprioritised by C-Suite executives. However, the consequences of ignoring this extreme risk are far-reaching, given the systemic ripple effects such a scenario would unleash. To bolster preparedness, FIIFs should:

Incorporate Interdisciplinary Knowledge: *Use behavioural sciences to anticipate panic, study financial history to recognise patterns and understand international law to navigate cross-border shocks.*
Simulate Extreme Scenarios: *Stress-test portfolios against unprecedented conditions, not just historical precedents.*
Create Contingency Playbooks: *Develop clear, actionable plans to address sudden liquidity crunches or valuation collapses.*

Monitor Non-Traditional Risks: *Assess the robustness of institutions, frameworks and assumptions that underpin financial systems.*

Survival vs. Oblivion
For an FIIF, the absence of an ERM plan tailored to extreme events can be the difference between survival and demise. Preparing for the USD's hypothetical downfall or any other global black swan is not just prudent but essential. In the chaotic world of finance, as with Edmond Dantès in *The Count of Monte Cristo*, survival is often about anticipating treachery, mastering strategy and acting decisively when the unexpected strikes.

PSYCHOLOGY AND CULTURE
Complacency often fosters inertia, dulling the readiness of portfolio managers and organisations to react decisively when crises emerge. The downfall of entities like Long-Term Capital Management (LTCM) and Lehman Brothers offers stark lessons on the dangers of overconfidence and weak risk cultures. LTCM's reliance on mathematical models blinded them to unquantifiable risks, while Lehman's management, as lamented by its former chief risk officer, lacked an appetite for rigorous risk oversight. These psychological and cultural shortcomings, more than external forces, sealed their fate.

Similarly, the widespread dismissal of the possibility of the USD losing its reserve currency status mirrors this dangerous complacency. Many financial professionals perceive this scenario as so remote that they neglect to develop contingency plans or stress-test their portfolios for such an eventuality. This mindset, rooted in overconfidence, mirrors the hubris of past failures.

Lessons from FC Barcelona's Set-Plays
A counterpoint to complacency can be drawn from FC Barcelona's meticulous preparation for set-plays in football. Every player is drilled repeatedly on their role in executing free kicks and corner routines, ensuring flawless coordination during matches. This systematic rehearsal transforms strategy into instinct, enabling decisive action under pressure. The same principle applies to financial institutions. Regular "set-play" drills simulating extreme scenarios, such as a sudden USD collapse, can embed response strategies into the organisational psyche.

Structured technical training can impart knowledge, but psychological readiness requires mental conditioning and a risk-conscious culture. Practicing emergency responses reinforces habits and sharpens instincts, preparing managers and institutions to act swiftly and effectively in a crisis.

Overcoming Organisational Inertia
Large FIIFs face additional challenges due to their complex structures, global operations and varied cultural and jurisdictional nuances. This complexity makes crafting coherent Extreme Risk Mitigation (ERM) plans daunting, increasing systemic vulnerabilities. Overcoming inertia requires viewing Business Continuity Plans (BCPs) as subsets of a broader, integrated ERM framework.

The "Titanic" Analogy [6]
The RMS Titanic, famously deemed "practically unsinkable," tragically sank on its maiden voyage due to overconfidence, insufficient lifeboats and ignored warnings. Like the Titanic, the USD is widely viewed as invulnerable to losing its reserve currency status. Yet, should the unthinkable occur, the impact on FIIFs unprepared for such a shift could be catastrophic.

Warnings about the USD's vulnerability abound, much like the ice warnings received by the Titanic. However, without a shift in psychology and culture, FIIFs risk a similar fate, metaphorically colliding with the "USD iceberg". Developing nimbleness and resilience through ERM plans and scenario testing is no longer optional, it is essential.

Hubris as the Fatal Flaw

The hubris that permeated Lehman Brothers, where management believed they knew better than everyone else, mirrors attitudes in many institutions today. Dismissing the potential collapse of the USD as improbable could lead to FIIFs being blindsided, much like the Titanic and Lehman were by their respective disasters.

The Call to Action

FIIFs must heed the warnings and adopt a proactive mindset. Regular scenario drills, a commitment to organisational agility, and fostering a culture of humility and preparedness can transform the "unthinkable" into a manageable challenge. Without such measures, FIIFs risk being crushed under the stampede of the "USD Elephant in the room."

SYSTEMIC RISK AGGREGATION UPSTREAM ("SYRAUP")

The concept of systemic risk aggregation upstream, or "syraup," describes a scenario where the aggregation of risks through multiple levels of fund management results in a concentration of exposure, rather than the intended diversification. Here's how this works:

Imagine a small fund manager who allocates some of its funds with a mid-sized fund manager. In turn, the mid-sized fund manager invests both the accumulated funds and its own capital into an even larger, reputable fund manager. This larger fund manager is trusted due to its established reputation and ability to manage funds for multiple clients, including other fund managers. The small and mid-sized fund managers believe that by outsourcing a portion of their funds to the larger manager, they are diversifying their investments. However, the funds are essentially becoming concentrated in the same investment, as the risk from all levels of the investment chain is aggregated upstream.

Further complicating matters, the individual investors who originally entrusted their funds to the small and mid-sized managers might themselves also be invested in the shares of the larger fund manager. This creates a recursive risk aggregation where funds, intended to be diversified, are increasingly concentrated in the same ~~large manager or~~ asset class, amplifying exposure instead of mitigating it. The unintended result is a systemic risk build-up, where a shock to the larger fund manager could cascade down through the entire hierarchy, leading to a significant collective loss across all levels.

Implications for the Fund Management Industry

This upstream aggregation of risk is particularly concerning in the context of the USD's potential decline in value or "demise." Given that the majority of assets in the global financial system are denominated in USD, this risk aggregation effect will be even more pronounced. As various fund managers (small, medium and large) invest in USD-denominated assets or funds, they inadvertently increase their exposure to USD-related risks.

If the USD faces a sharp devaluation, the effects could be catastrophic for these fund managers, especially since they all hold overlapping positions. The "exit door" for USD-denominated assets would be narrow, with too many investors trying to offload their holdings at once. In such a panic, the market may become illiquid and there may be a lack of buyers, making it even harder for investors to sell their assets without incurring significant losses.

The Potential Crisis: Herd Behaviour and Lack of Buyers

In the case of a widespread rush to exit USD-denominated assets, market participants could face the real risk of having to "pay" counterparties to take over their positions, essentially paying for someone to buy their assets, which sounds absurd but has historical precedence.

For example, the Bank of Japan (BOJ) introduced negative interest rates in 2016 to counteract the rising value of the Yen and combat deflation. In such an environment, depositors were charged to hold their funds at the central bank, rather than being paid interest, leading to a situation that many would have previously considered impossible. The negative interest rate policy was controversial and difficult to comprehend, yet it happened. Similarly, in the case of the USD demise, financial markets could face equally irrational scenarios where traditional market dynamics no longer apply.

Historical Precedents and the Risks of Illiquidity

The BOJ's negative interest rate policy highlights the potential for financial systems to behave in unexpected and counterintuitive ways during extreme conditions. Just as Mrs. Watanabe, the iconic frugal Japanese housewife, preferred to keep her money in a biscuit tin rather than pay the BOJ for the privilege of holding funds, investors in a USD collapse scenario might panic and hoard assets, worsening liquidity problems.

This phenomenon underscores the risks of over-concentration of investments in a single asset class or currency (in this case, USD). When the market turns sour, a systemic risk chain reaction may occur, leading to widespread losses and further exacerbating the crisis. Investors and fund managers alike must be aware of these risks and consider how they might mitigate them.

Concentration through "Syraup"

The systemic aggregation of risk upstream (syraup) is a critical but often overlooked factor in investment management. When fund managers inadvertently concentrate their exposure to the same asset or market through layered investments, they increase the systemic risk faced by the entire chain of investment. The potential demise of the USD as the world's reserve currency could expose this risk in a dramatic way, with financial institutions and individuals alike facing the consequences of illiquidity, panic selling and a dearth of buyers. To avoid such outcomes, the focus must be on genuine diversification, risk mitigation and preparing for extreme scenarios that challenge even the most established financial assumptions.

RHYTHMS IN FINANCIAL MARKETS

The phrase *"This time is different"* is often invoked during periods of optimism or when financial innovations or new trends emerge. However, history has shown that this overconfidence can quickly turn to regret when market dynamics change, revealing that "this time is no different." The rhythm of financial markets, driven by speculative fads, innovations, and cycles of boom and bust, often leads to complacency followed by catastrophic losses. This cyclical pattern reflects human nature, market behaviour, and the inherent volatility within financial systems.

The "This Time is Different" Fallacy

Throughout history, financial crises and market collapses have been preceded by the belief that the current situation is unique, that it is different from the past and that previous lessons no longer apply. This false sense of security is often bolstered by new financial innovations or market trends, which seem to promise unprecedented growth. When these trends inevitably falter, the realisation sets in that, in fact, "this time is no different."

Regulatory bodies have long struggled with controlling the flow of speculative capital across jurisdictions, especially when it involves the USD, the world's dominant reserve currency. The free-flowing nature of capital, coupled with limited oversight, creates fertile ground for bubbles, herd behaviour and the rapid inflows and outflows of funds into new, sometimes unproven financial innovations. While the Federal Reserve under

Alan Greenspan once suggested that financial innovations were an antidote to inflation, this view was soon challenged when asset prices ballooned, fuelling inflationary pressures instead. The ongoing clash between optimism for new financial trends and the recognition of past patterns, "this time is different versus no different at all" creates cyclical rhythms in the financial markets.

Speculative Bets and their Fallout
Two notable examples of such cycles of boom and bust include the cases of *Amaranth Advisors and Archegos Capital Management*, both of which illustrate the dangers of speculative investments and the aggregation of risk upstream (syraup).

Amaranth Advisors (2006): Amaranth Advisors, at one point managing USD 9 billion in assets, suffered a colossal $5 billion loss when its speculative bets on natural gas futures went awry. The firm's strategy involved highly leveraged positions in natural gas markets, which ultimately led to its downfall. Amaranth was later charged by the Commodity Futures Trading Commission (CFTC) for market manipulation, and many of its investors were left with massive losses. This case highlights how speculative trends driven by short-term gains can lead to catastrophic outcomes when risks are not properly managed. [7]

Archegos Capital Management (2021): Archegos, a family office founded by Bill Hwang, collapsed in March 2021, after making highly leveraged bets on U.S. equities. The firm was reported to be leveraged up to five times when it incurred a staggering $30 billion loss on liquidated positions. Archegos was exposed to a concentrated set of positions and when the bets went wrong, the firm could not meet its margin calls. The fallout was significant, causing severe losses at financial institutions like *Nomura, Credit Suisse, Goldman Sachs* and *Morgan Stanley*. Credit Suisse alone lost USD 5.5 billion, which played a role in the bank's eventual collapse and forced merger with UBS. The Archegos episode is a prime example of risk aggregation where multiple financial institutions piled into similar positions, exacerbating the consequences when the bets failed.

Tell Tale signs of "Syraup"
The Archegos disaster exemplified the *systemic risk aggregation upstream (syraup)* effect, where multiple financial institutions, believing they were diversifying their investments by trusting a reputable fund manager, unknowingly concentrated their risks. In the case of Archegos, many fund managers and banks that invested in the fund or in its assets believed they were diversifying their portfolios by outsourcing a portion of their capital to a trusted player. In reality, they were all exposed to the same risk, leading to massive losses when the fund's strategy collapsed.

The Rhythm of Financial Crises
The emergence of these trends whether speculative investments, financial innovations or even financial products often occurs in rhythmic cycles. Markets experience peaks of euphoric growth followed by troughs of panic and liquidation. These cycles are driven by human behaviour, the search for higher returns and the belief that "this time is different." The past is often ignored and risks are underestimated until it is too late.

The financial system's capacity to absorb these shocks can vary depending on the depth of risk aggregation. As seen with the collapse of Archegos and Amaranth, the risk aggregation effect can make these financial crises more severe. The more institutions, funds and individual investors aggregate risk into the same positions, the more likely they are to experience contagion and systemic collapse when the bubble bursts.

How different is this time?

The cycles of financial innovation, speculative trends and risk aggregation contribute to the rhythmic nature of financial markets. While each new cycle may be touted as a unique opportunity ("this time is different"), history has shown that the risks and outcomes are often strikingly similar. Speculative bets, unhedged exposures and systemic risk aggregation, such as in the cases of Amaranth Advisors and Archegos Capital Management, continue to expose the vulnerabilities of the global financial system. As financial institutions and investors move through these cycles, they must remain mindful of history's lessons and prepare for the inevitable rhythm of market disruptions. [8] [9]

SOVEREIGN NATIONS

The Global "Addiction" to the USD and its Implications for Central Banks and Sovereign Wealth Funds (SWFs)

The **USD's dominance** as the world's reserve currency is deeply entrenched, largely because of the characteristics it offers stability, liquidity and its central role in global trade. For many countries, this "addiction" to the USD is a practical necessity. Central banks hold USD in their reserves primarily for two reasons: first, because the U.S. is often a major trading partner, and second, as part of a currency basket they need to periodically rebalance. Moreover, central banks use reserves to regulate their money supply and manage exchange rates, often intervening to defend the value of their currencies within targeted trading bands.

Given the global prominence of the USD, many central banks are faced with a dilemma. While holding USD is essential for economic stability and trade facilitation, it also exposes nations to significant risks, particularly in times of USD depreciation or a crisis of confidence in the U.S. Dollar system.

THE ROLE OF SOVEREIGN WEALTH FUNDS (SWFs)

To avoid overcomplicating the central bank's mission of managing domestic monetary policy, many affluent countries have set up **Sovereign Wealth Funds (SWFs)**. These are large, government-owned investment funds typically designed to manage national savings or foreign reserves. Some of the most notable SWFs include:

Norway: Government Pension Fund of Norway
Saudi Arabia: Public Investment Fund (PIF)
Qatar: Qatar Investment Authority (QIA)
UAE: Abu Dhabi Investment Authority (ADIA)
Singapore: Government Investment Corporation (GIC) and Temasek Holdings

These funds serve as a form of financial buffer and diversification. They have mandates to generate returns from global investments, not just to safeguard reserves. Much like **Financial Institutions and Investment Firms (FIIFs)**, SWFs can face similar risks, such as *"this time is different"* thinking and speculative behaviour.

Despite their sophistication, SWFs are not immune to market extremes and fluctuations, including the possibility of a significant fall in the value of the USD, which could severely affect their portfolios. Given their substantial assets under management (AUM), SWFs, much like FIIFs, must navigate the global economic landscape with caution.

Currency Exposure and National-Level Monitoring

A significant challenge for nations holding USD in their reserves is the **currency exposure** it entails. As the world's reserve currency, the USD is deeply embedded in global financial systems. However, such dependence creates risks. For instance, a dramatic shift in the value of the USD (due to a loss of confidence or a systemic financial crisis) could trigger a cascade of effects across countries and markets.

To avoid this **systemic risk aggregation upstream** (syraup), countries must carefully manage their currency exposure and prepare strategically. One key lesson from history is how **Singapore's First Finance Minister** quietly increased the nation's gold reserves during periods of heightened uncertainty (see page xx). This **gold diversification** strategy is a way to hedge against the potential fall of the USD. In fact, several countries, including **China, Poland and Singapore,** made substantial increases in their gold reserves in 2023, signalling a broader shift in global reserve management. (See Table 6a)

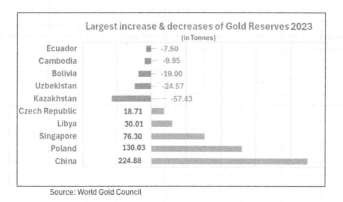

Source: World Gold Council

Figure 6a: *China, Poland and Singapore were the largest increase in Gold Reserves in2023*

Domestic Preparations to Cushion the Shocks of USD Demise

To mitigate the risks associated with a USD collapse, countries must also strengthen **domestic resilience**. This involves:

Fiscal Discipline: Governments should focus on prudent public spending and building **sustainable sources of revenue** to withstand external shocks.
Strong Economic Institutions: Countries with robust, well-regulated financial institutions with a **global network of relationships** are more likely to remain attractive to international investors and be resilient in times of crisis.
Think-Tanks and Innovation: As centres for new ideas and policies, **think-tanks** can help governments anticipate and mitigate economic challenges. In particular, think-tanks provide an invaluable forum for developing alternative economic frameworks, solutions to regional or global problems and collaborative strategies with other nations.

Foreign-Focused Strategies to Diversify Away from the USD
In addition to domestic strategies, countries must also look outward for ways to reduce their reliance on the USD. Some potential strategies include:

Currency Swaps and Liquidity Pools: Nations can arrange **currency swap agreements** with trading partners to facilitate international trade without using USD as an intermediary. Furthermore, countries can establish **trade agreements** that use local currencies instead of the USD for cross-border transactions, thus decreasing the USD's centrality in global trade. Countries could collaborate to establish **regional liquidity pools**, ensuring that in times of currency crisis, they don't have to rely on the USD as a safe-haven asset. These pools could provide critical liquidity during periods of uncertainty.

Digital Currency and Cross-Border Payments: The rise of **Central Bank Digital Currencies (CBDCs)** and **digital payment systems** provides an opportunity for nations to bypass traditional USD-based systems. By establishing cross-border payment platforms independent of the **SWIFT network** or U.S.-based clearing systems, countries could facilitate smoother international transactions.

Military and Regional Security Cooperation: To safeguard economic interests, **military collaboration** and **regional security agreements** are essential. Stable, secure trade routes free from conflict or piracy ensure the free movement of goods and services without disruption.

Enhancing the Think-Tank Ecosystem: **Think-tanks** are integral in shaping policy responses to economic and financial challenges. They generate ideas, conduct research and provide critical analyses of global and domestic issues. The **Brookings Institution** [10] is a prime example of such an organisation. In June 2022, it hosted a panel discussion on the future of the USD, examining whether the USD's position as the world's dominant currency was sustainable. This type of think-tank ecosystem focused on **research, innovation and collaboration** helps countries better navigate economic transitions, including the possibility of a USD collapse.

Strategic Diversification and Collaboration

The **USD's dominance** presents both opportunities and risks. While its position as the world's reserve currency has provided stability, it also creates vulnerabilities. As nations anticipate potential shifts in global power dynamics, particularly in light of digital currency initiatives, increasing gold reserves and alternative trading systems, they must act proactively. By strengthening fiscal discipline, building robust economic institutions and fostering international collaboration, countries can better manage their overdependence on the USD and navigate future economic uncertainties.

POLITICAL LEADERSHIP

As a student studying aeronautical engineering at Imperial College in 1985, I vividly remember watching a live televised U.K. Parliament session at the House of Commons. A lady dressed in blue with an immaculate hairdo rose from her seat to respond to the opposition's comments. With fluency and precision, she interspersed facts with wit and humour, cutting through the din of opposition hecklers and invoking a chorus of laughter from the Tory backbenchers. That lady was Margaret Thatcher.

Margaret Thatcher inherited a crumbling economy when she became the U.K.'s first female Prime Minister in 1979. Her push for the privatisation of nationalised industries paid dividends for both her and the Conservative Party. Her decisiveness and tenacity as a leader were particularly evident when she acted without hesitation, sending British naval forces to reclaim control of the Falkland Islands from the Argentine Military Junta, which had invaded them without warning.

She also faced and ultimately defeated the National Union of Mineworkers (NUM), led by the militant Arthur Scargill, who resisted the closure of unprofitable coal mines that were draining government coffers. Thatcher subdued the strike-prone labour unions, shut down unproductive collieries and promoted homeownership. She boosted U.K. labour productivity growth and reshaped the nation's economic landscape.

Thatcher firmly believed that economic freedom and individual liberty were interdependent. She argued that a nation's prosperity could only be achieved through personal responsibility and hard work. Her strong stance against aggression from Russia earned her the nickname *"The Iron Lady"* from the Soviet press. When she first took office, she declared that her goal was to turn Britain from a "dependent" society into a self-reliant one, from a "give-it-to-me" nation into a "do-it-yourself" one.

In a speech, against the opposition of even her own Conservative Party members, she famously remarked: "I am not a consensus politician, I am a conviction politician." Indeed, Margaret Thatcher's leadership, defined by her steadfast convictions, transformed modern Britain. [11]

Heading east, Singapore's founding father, **Lee Kuan Yew**, transformed the nation from swamplands into a bustling metropolis within a single generation. His leadership was marked by an insatiable appetite for learning, a zero-tolerance policy toward corruption, a pragmatic approach to problem-solving and an iron-willed resolve to make tough decisions—traits that earned him admiration from many.

In his famous speech at an election rally on 19 December 1980, Lee recounted an incident in which he put a stop to an illegal work-to-rule industrial action launched by the Singapore Airlines Pilots' Association (SIAPA). The pilots had demanded a 30% salary increase and better working conditions. Speaking in the rain, Lee recalled confronting the SIAPA leaders with two choices: stop the intimidation, return to work, restore discipline and then argue their case with the government, or if they continued with their agitation, and Lee would "teach them a lesson they would never forget." He made it clear that he was prepared to start the national airline all over again without them. Faced with such unwavering resolve, SIAPA retreated and the industrial action came to an immediate end. Lee Kuan Yew had won.

At that rally, he went on to deliver his famous line: *"Whoever governs Singapore must have the iron in him. Or give it up. This is not a game of cards. This is your life and mine. I spent a whole lifetime building this. And as long as I'm in charge, nobody is going to knock it down."* This moment encapsulates the determined, no-nonsense and iron-willed leadership that defined Lee Kuan Yew, a leader whose political resolve left an indelible mark on Singapore's history. [12]

One of China's most prominent leaders, **Deng Xiaoping**, is widely credited with opening China to the world and initiating a series of transformative reforms that reshaped the nation's economic policies. Under his leadership, China strengthened its trade and cultural ties with the West and Chinese enterprises were opened to foreign investment, marking a new era for the country. Many historians regard Deng as the leader who began to transform the face of modern China.

Deng's focus on the "four modernisations"—economy, agriculture, science and technology, and defence—catalysed significant progress, turning China into the manufacturing powerhouse it is today. His policies not only propelled China's industrialisation but also lifted more than a fifty to sixty percent of its population out of poverty. Deng's openness to new ideas and his pragmatic approach in pursuing his vision were the keys to his success. He was not constrained by strict communist ideology and was willing to embrace whatever worked, regardless of its origins. This pragmatism was famously encapsulated in his old proverb: *"It does not matter if a cat is black or white, as long as it catches mice, it is a good cat."*

A visionary and practical leader, Deng Xiaoping's reforms laid the groundwork for China's rise on the global stage, marking him as one of the most significant figures in the country's modern history. [13]

Richard Nixon's historic visit to China in 1972 marked a pivotal moment in Sino-American relations, fundamentally altering the trajectory of both countries' diplomatic, economic and cultural exchanges. At the time, such a request from a Western leader to visit China was unprecedented. It was especially surprising given the pressing issues the Western world was grappling with: economic stagnation, rising inflation and the tense backdrop of the Cold War. Nixon's visit, however, helped break the ice, thawing decades of strained relations between China and the U.S. and setting the stage for a new era of engagement.

This visit paved the way for major shifts in global diplomacy. Just a year later, China was admitted to the United Nations, assuming Taiwan's seat as a permanent member of the UN Security Council. Nixon's groundbreaking outreach to China led to a thaw in relations that would only grow in significance. In 1979, when Deng Xiaoping met with U.S. President Jimmy Carter to formally normalise diplomatic relations, he insisted that Richard Nixon be present at the White House meeting. This gesture was a clear acknowledgment of Nixon's pivotal role in bridging the gap between the two nations, solidifying his place in history as a key architect of China-U.S. rapprochement.

Nixon's bold move to break from twenty years of U.S. isolationist policy towards China required immense political courage, especially considering previous administrations had refused to recognise the People's Republic of China due to its communist ideology. But Nixon, with his visionary approach, initiated this diplomatic breakthrough, demonstrating both boldness and humility in setting aside Cold War animosities to pursue a more constructive future.

As Nixon once said, *"The greatest honour history can bestow is that of peacemaker"*. His role in re-establishing China-U.S. relations, fostering trade and promoting global dialogue underscored his enduring legacy as a peacemaker who reshaped the international landscape. [14]

It is virtually impossible to fully encapsulate the achievements and attributes of these four leaders, and this, I believe, is well understood. The primary purpose here is to demonstrate that all four leaders showcased remarkable courage, pragmatism and an unwavering willingness to make tough yet necessary decisions for the betterment of their people. Each of them, in their own way, endured the horrors of war, confronted ideological clashes and persevered to drive the societal changes that would transform their nations. Political leadership, therefore, stands as the key catalyst that can facilitate the other factors discussed in the "Sovereign Nations" section.

In addressing the *"USD Elephant in the Room"*, it will take immense political will, courage, pragmatism and wisdom to adopt a proactive *"Prepare and Act"* approach, rather than merely maintaining the passive *"Wait and Hope"* status quo. The brief exploration of these four leaders' legacies reinforces the critical message that political leaders must not shy away from making difficult decisions and must possess the foresight to prepare for the eventual reckoning of the USD. *What can be done now, must be done soon.*

MAJOR FINANCIAL CENTRES

The world's major financial centres are distributed across key regions. In the Western hemisphere, New York, London, Paris and Frankfurt dominate. In the Eastern half, Tokyo, Singapore, Hong Kong and Shanghai stand out. In the Middle East, cities like Dubai, Abu Dhabi, Riyadh and Doha act as financial hubs, largely driven by their sovereign wealth funds (SWFs).

If the USD maintains its dominance as the global reserve currency, key exchanges such as Euronext Paris, Frankfurt Exchange, London Stock Exchange, Chicago Board of Trade, Chicago Mercantile Exchange, New York Stock Exchange and Nasdaq will continue to operate in a "business-as-usual" mode. This status quo benefits these cities, allowing them to remain central to global finance. Many sovereign wealth funds (SWFs) and financial institutions (FIIFs) have offices in these locations to execute trades, manage investments and mitigate risks. These cities will likely continue thriving as major financial hubs for global markets and international trade.

From the late 1980s to the early 1990s, Tokyo was the primary financial hub in Asia, attracting global investors with Japanese equities. Foreign exchange (FX) currency futures, Euroyen and Eurodollar interest-rate futures were actively traded on the Tokyo Stock Exchange (TSE) and Tokyo International Financial Futures Exchange (TIFFE). However, when the Japanese "bubble" burst, attention shifted to the "Asian Tigers" of Korea, Thailand, Malaysia, Indonesia and Singapore. This period marked the rise of Hong Kong and Singapore as prominent financial centres in Asia. With China's opening, Shanghai too, emerged as a significant financial hub. This shift explains how Asia came to host Tokyo, Shanghai, Hong Kong and Singapore as major financial centres.

Impact of the Decline of USD in International Trade
But what will happen if the USD loses its position as the world's dominant currency? Such a shift would require significant catalysts, possibly a drastic reduction in U.S. trade relations with the rest of the world or a decline in the attractiveness of U.S. financial assets due to structural issues like rising fiscal deficits and national debt. A decrease in global financial activity and trade stemming from the reduced popularity of the USD could lower trading volumes and business activity, potentially diminishing the importance of New York and London as global financial centres.

In this scenario, if multiple currencies were to emerge as alternatives in international finance and trade, the impact on other major financial centres beyond New York and London might be less significant. The need for investment and business would continue, and talent would remain attracted to existing hubs. However, if Central Bank Digital Currencies (CBDCs) are fully realised, [15] the need for traditional financial centres could decrease, as international trade and finance shift toward decentralised, digital platforms. This decentralisation aligns with the principles of digital currencies.

Under a multiple-currency or CBDC scenario, Singapore would likely continue to thrive due to its strong governance, business-friendly environment, rule of law and robust infrastructure. Middle Eastern cities, which are at the forefront of digital currencies and fintech, might also benefit, bolstered by their tax-friendly policies.

Emergence of RMB or Other Currencies

If the RMB were to replace the USD as the dominant global currency, Shanghai could rise to prominence. The global shift toward RMB would likely lead to a diversion of funds from Singapore and Hong Kong toward Shanghai, as international trade and finance are increasingly conducted in RMB. This shift would result in a decrease in Singapore's Assets Under Management (AUM) and demand for its financial services would decline. Talent would likely migrate northwards to Shanghai and Hong Kong, leading to a reduction in Singapore's financial activity coupled with a broader economic contraction.

Given that Hong Kong is closely tied to China, it would benefit from the rise of the RMB, reaffirming its status as the "Gateway to China." To ensure RMB liquidity across time zones, China may designate a Middle Eastern and a European city to facilitate RMB settlement and clearing. Riyadh, with its strong energy ties to China, could benefit, while Paris and Frankfurt would compete for the role of European financial hubs for RMB-related services.

The EUR Scenario

If the EUR were to ascend as the global reserve currency, European cities like London, Paris and Frankfurt would increase in importance. In this case, the impact on Asian financial centres would likely be less significant. The demand for EUR would drive finance toward European hubs, but Asian centres would remain relevant in global finance.

The Role of Political, Economic, and Military (PoEM) Pillars

For any currency to rise to global dominance, its nation would need to demonstrate substantial progress in the Political, Economic and Military (PoEM) pillars outlined earlier in this book. Political leadership, economic influence and military power are all crucial in shaping the global financial order. The country whose currency reigns supreme would exert considerable influence over international trade and finance, just as the United States has with the USD.

Thus, the future of financial centres in the event of the USD's dethronement presents a complex and unpredictable scenario. Political leadership, continuous innovation and the ability to adapt to global changes will determine the future relevance of each financial hub. The disruption to the global financial landscape will demand bold action. In this new environment, "survival of the fittest" will not be enough; it will be "survival of the most prepared."

UNDERSTANDING THE DEMISE OF THE USD: CURRENCY CONTENDERS

To anticipate how the demise of the USD could unfold, it is crucial to evaluate the strengths and weaknesses of the potential currency contenders. In a world inundated with propaganda, opinions and misinformation, it is essential to focus on what has already

been accomplished, rather than solely listening to critics about what remains to be done. As the renowned scientist Marie Curie once said:
"One never notices what has been done; one can only see what remains to be done."
This reminder underscores the importance of recognising progress while acknowledging the ongoing work needed for the future.

Central Bank Digital Currencies (CBDCs)

CBDCs are credible contenders for the role of the world's reserve currency. Numerous central banks have initiated projects exploring digital currency technologies. While the technology is advancing quickly, the regulatory, security and operational aspects of CBDCs require substantial development. For CBDCs to gain widespread adoption as reserve currencies, it will take careful attention not only to the technological infrastructure but also to the regulatory frameworks that govern their use. Much work remains to be done in these areas.

Japanese Yen (JPY)

In the 1980s, as Japan's economy surged, many predicted that the Japanese Yen (JPY) would soon challenge the dominance of the USD as the world's leading currency. However, the bursting of Japan's economic bubble silenced such forecasts. Despite this setback, the JPY remains a significant player in the global financial landscape, supported by Japan's strong economic foundations and international influence.

The JPY's strengths are manifold. It enjoys widespread acceptance in global trade and finance, reflecting international confidence in Japan's economic stability. Japan's well-developed and liquid fixed-income markets, particularly those denominated in JPY, attract substantial global investment. Moreover, Japanese equities benefit from extensive international exposure, demonstrating Japan's integration into the global economy. As a member of the G7, Japan also wields influence in shaping global economic policies, adding to the JPY's credibility. Historically, Japan's status as the world's second-largest economy for decades, only recently overtaken by China, has further bolstered its economic stature.

However, the JPY faces notable challenges. The Bank of Japan's (BOJ) large-scale purchases of Japanese Government Bonds (JGBs) and Exchange-Traded Funds (ETFs) have raised concerns about excessive government debt and potential distortions in financial markets, undermining confidence in the currency's stability. Additionally, Japan's cautious approach to global political leadership limits its ability to assert greater influence on the world stage, which could constrain the JPY's potential to achieve a more dominant status in international finance.

While the JPY may not currently rival the USD as a global reserve currency, it remains a cornerstone of the international financial system. By addressing its domestic financial imbalances and adopting a more proactive role in global affairs, Japan could enhance the JPY's significance and influence in the evolving global economic landscape.

Euro (EUR)

Introduced in January 1999, the Euro (EUR) has gradually established itself as a formidable global currency, with more European countries adopting it over time. Managed by the European Central Bank (ECB), the Euro is now a key player in international finance, widely held in global central bank reserves. The Eurozone, comprising the countries that use the currency, also benefits from a political union through the European Parliament and military cooperation via NATO, further bolstering its global influence.

The EUR's strengths are significant. As a large and unified political and economic entity, the Eurozone has substantial bargaining power on the global stage, enabling it to negotiate favourable trade terms with other nations. Additionally, the EUR holds the position of the second-most widely held currency in global central bank reserves, a testament to its credibility and the confidence placed in the region's financial stability.

However, the EUR also faces challenges. While the Eurozone has a common monetary policy, individual member countries maintain their own fiscal policies. This lack of fiscal unity introduces the risk that national policies could conflict with broader monetary strategies, undermining the currency's stability. Moreover, economic disparities between Eurozone countries persist, with some nations experiencing slower growth and development. Over the past decade, labour productivity growth within the region has stagnated, which has limited the EUR's potential for further appreciation and its ability to challenge the dominance of other global currencies like the USD.

While the EUR remains a strong contender in the global currency landscape, its future strength will depend on addressing internal economic disparities and aligning fiscal policies across the Eurozone to ensure sustained stability and growth.

Chinese Renminbi (RMB)

The Renminbi (RMB) has several merits that position it as a potential contender to challenge the dominance of the U.S. Dollar. One key factor is that RMB transactions can now be settled through the Cross-Border Payment System (CIPS), a significant step toward internationalising the currency. China's vast foreign exchange reserves, totalling approximately USD 3.1 trillion, provide substantial backing for the RMB's stability. Furthermore, China holds around 2,113 metric tons of gold, making it one of the largest official gold holders globally, which strengthens its financial position.

However, the RMB faces significant hurdles in its quest to become a global reserve currency. Capital controls and an unliberalised capital account limit the free flow of capital, which remains a major obstacle to the RMB's international standing. While China has made strides in developing a robust financial structure, it still needs to build more political credibility as a responsible leader in international finance. Demonstrating consistent, market-friendly policies will be crucial for enhancing global trust in the RMB.

Despite these challenges, the gradual liberalisation of China's capital account could significantly enhance the RMB's potential as a global reserve currency, positioning it to challenge the USD in the long run. As Curie's quote reminds us, China is aware of the necessary reforms and is focused on addressing the remaining barriers.

As we consider the potential contenders for a post-USD global currency system, it becomes evident that each option carries its own strengths and challenges. Central Bank Digital Currencies (CBDCs) represent an emerging possibility, while currencies like the Japanese Yen (JPY), the Euro (EUR) and the Renminbi (RMB) each present unique advantages and obstacles. The transition away from the USD as the global reserve currency will likely be gradual, involving significant economic and political shifts. Understanding these contenders' attributes will help us better assess the feasibility of such a transition. The road ahead is complex and much work remains to be done.

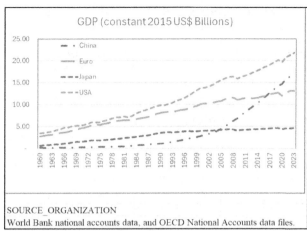

Figure 6b: *United States, China, EU and Japan GDP comparisons. In 2023, GDP figures in USD Trillions:*
*United States **21.78**, China **17.17**, EU **13.1**, Japan **4.62***

Foreign exchange reserves as of the end of 2021 of the top four countries provide a numerical perspective of how far ahead China is in terms of reserves being held.

China	USD 3.3 trillion
	(excluding Hong Kong's USD 496.8 billion and Taiwan's USD 548.4 billion)
Japan	USD 1.3 trillion
Switzerland	USD 1 trillion
India	USD 0.569.9 trillion

Sources: *State Administration of Foreign Exchange of the People's Republic of China, Hong Kong Monetary Authority, Taiwan's central bank, Japanese Ministry of Finance, Swiss National Bank, Reserve Bank of India.*

From observing the GDP trajectory in Figure 6b and the foreign reserves figures, it is mathematically probable for China's GDP to surpass that of U.S. before 2050. From a foreign reserves' consideration, RMB is in pole to become a reserve currency of the world if USD continues to stumble on its own foibles.

POSSIBLE SCENARIOS FOR THE DEMISE OF THE USD AS THE WORLD'S RESERVE CURRENCY

If the USD were to lose its status as the world's reserve currency, the economic consequences would be far-reaching, impacting not only the United States but also the global economy. Below are several possible scenarios, though not exhaustive, that explore potential outcomes and responses from market participants.

BASKET OF CURRENCIES SCENARIO

In the not-too-distant future, the global financial system begins to experience a seismic shift. For decades, the U.S. Dollar (USD) had reigned supreme as the world's reserve currency, the linchpin of international trade and finance. But the economic landscape had started to change. Countries, tired of the risks associated with relying too heavily on the USD, began to explore alternatives. Soon, whispers of a new global system grew louder, one in which the USD was no longer the sole dominant currency.

A growing consensus began to take shape: the future of global trade might lie in a basket of currencies. The EUR, RMB, JPY and other regional currencies started to make their case. Central banks, long reliant on the stability of the USD, now found themselves faced with the daunting task of managing a more diverse portfolio of reserves. The days of simply holding vast sums of U.S. Treasury bonds and USD were over. Countries had to adapt to this new multi-currency world and the operational complexity was immediately apparent.

Central banks were no longer just managing the risks of the USD. Now, they had to track fluctuations in the value of multiple currencies, each subject to its own forces and volatility. The familiar rhythm of USD price discovery, once the bedrock of international trade, began to falter. Exchange rates, once relatively stable under the dominance of the USD, began to lurch unpredictably as markets adjusted to the new reality. With the absence of a single currency to anchor trade, global markets began to experience wild swings, complicating everything from investment strategies to international contracts.

The effects on international trade were immediate and far-reaching. Without the steady presence of a universally accepted currency, businesses found themselves grappling with the new uncertainty. The cost of cross-border transactions soared as companies had to manage the risks of fluctuating exchange rates, making international deals more expensive and less predictable. Trade volumes, once flowing freely through the well-oiled machinery of USD-denominated transactions, began to decline. In this new world, trade became a far more complicated affair and with it came the spectre of inflation. As prices for goods and services began to rise across borders, consumers around the world felt the pain. Economies, especially those in emerging markets, found themselves squeezed as the cost of living increased while trade slowed.

In the face of these challenges, nations began to form new alliances. As the complexities of dealing with a basket of currencies grew, countries sought refuge in trading blocs. These blocs would offer a way to stabilise trade within their borders, using agreed-upon reference baskets and standardised protocols for transactions. Countries grouped together, driven not only by geographic proximity but also by shared economic interests, such as common currencies or economic policies. These new alliances reshaped the global order, as nations realigned themselves around currencies other than the USD, included the EUR, RMB and JPY.

The implications of this shift were profound. The United States, long the central player in global economic governance, found its influence waning. With countries forming their own economic groupings around the EUR, RMB and JPY, the U.S. lost its leverage over global trade agreements. The dominance that had once been ensured by the USD's status as the world's reserve currency seemed like a distant memory.

Meanwhile, the World Trade Organisation (WTO) scrambled to adapt its framework to accommodate this multi-currency environment. The once-clear guidelines for global trade needed to be restructured. New settlement practices had to be standardised to ensure that goods and commodities could still be traded efficiently despite the multiplicity of currencies in use. The WTO, once a stabilising force in a USD-dominated world, found itself rethinking the global trading system.

As this new financial order took shape, the world was left to reckon with the consequences of a fragmented currency system. While the shift brought about opportunities for diversification and reduced reliance on the USD, it also created a landscape fraught with volatility, uncertainty and rising costs. The globe, once comfortably anchored by the U.S. Dollar, was now navigating the complexities of a multi-currency world and the full implications of this transition would unfold in the years to come.

GLOBAL STABLE COINS AND CENTRAL BANK DIGITAL CURRENCIES SCENARIO

A profound shift unfolds in the global financial landscape. The once-dominant USD, the bedrock of international trade and finance for decades, is gradually replaced by a new form of money: Global Stablecoins (GSCs). Backed by commodities like gold and silver, these digital currencies quickly gain traction in global trade, reducing the world's reliance on national currencies. For the first time in history, the world begins to experience the effects of a truly borderless, decentralised currency system.

But with this dramatic shift comes a set of unforeseen challenges. Central banks, long accustomed to controlling national monetary policy, find themselves losing their grip. The ability to influence inflation, interest rates and employment is no longer within their reach, as GSCs bypass traditional national currencies and financial systems. Governments, once the masters of their economic destinies, struggle to maintain control. They are confronted with a new era where their ability to stabilise their economies is weakened by the decentralised nature of these digital currencies.

This decentralisation is powered by blockchain technology, which promises to bring transparency and security to the global financial system. Yet, as global transactions shift to this new digital realm, regulatory bodies find themselves scrambling. The decentralised nature of GSCs, while efficient, makes it difficult to enforce anti-money laundering measures and other financial safeguards. Fraud, tax evasion and illicit financial activities become rampant as authorities struggle to track and manage the free flow of digital currencies. The risks of this new, unregulated frontier become more apparent with each passing day.

With GSCs now on the rise, countries across the world are confronted with another dilemma: the challenge of capital controls. Governments, once able to control the flow of money across borders, now find it nearly impossible to regulate the movement of digital assets. Speculative flows and sudden capital outflows wreak havoc on national economies, destabilising markets, especially in emerging economies that were once shielded from such volatility. The world's financial systems are caught in an intricate web and governments are forced to confront the complexities of this new, digital-first world.

In response to these growing concerns, central banks begin to issue their own digital currencies, Central Bank Digital Currencies (CBDCs). Unlike the decentralised GSCs, CBDCs are government-backed and centrally controlled, offering a more stable and secure alternative. Countries around the world work together to build an interconnected digital payments system that allows for seamless transactions across borders, bypassing the need for the USD and reducing the complexities of currency conversions.

The emergence of CBDCs offers a glimmer of hope. With governments now able to oversee these currencies, central banks regain control over monetary policy and financial regulations. Inflation is more easily managed, interest rates can be adjusted to stimulate economic growth and the threat of financial crime is minimised as CBDCs comply with national and international regulations. These digital currencies, fully backed by governments, become the preferred choice for businesses, consumers and governments alike.

As the global financial system shifts, the world begins to navigate the coexistence of GSCs and CBDCs. GSCs continue to operate as a decentralised, commodity-backed alternative, while CBDCs become the cornerstone of national economic policies, offering a safe, regulated framework for international trade. However, the transition is not without its challenges. The balance between innovation and regulation proves difficult to maintain. As countries, institutions and individuals adjust, the global financial system undergoes a massive transformation.

In this new world, the rise of digital currencies, both centralised and decentralised, ushers in a new era of financial complexity. Governments must adapt to a rapidly changing environment, balancing the need for innovation with the imperative of financial security. The outcome remains uncertain, but one thing is clear: the era of the USD as the sole global reserve currency is over, and a more diverse and fragmented financial landscape is emerging before our eyes.

USD FADES WITHOUT A SUCCESSOR SCENARIO

The year is 2030, and the global financial landscape is undergoing a seismic shift. The U.S. Dollar, once the bedrock of international trade and the world's dominant reserve currency, is beginning to lose its grip on the world stage. As we sit in a crowded financial district, the quiet hum of computers and screens belies the monumental changes unfolding around the globe. What was once an unshakeable foundation is now showing cracks and the implications are becoming increasingly apparent.

Countries like China and Russia, along with the other BRICS members, Brazil, India and South Africa, have begun to challenge the U.S.'s financial supremacy. The rise of the Chinese RMB as a global trade currency has gained traction, aided by the growing economic influence of China and its Belt and Road Initiative. In the background, BRICS is pushing for a more unified trading framework among its members, one that bypasses the need for the USD.

Across the globe, trade agreements are being rewritten. No longer is the world tethered to a single reserve currency; multiple systems of settlement and clearing are beginning to take shape. A Chinese-led financial network starts to gain ground and whispers of a BRICS-based trading system are becoming more than just talk. These alternative networks, while still in their infancy, are emerging alongside the USD-based system, creating a fragmented financial ecosystem.

The old familiar rhythms of global trade are starting to change. What was once a simple, uniform process of exchanging goods and services for USD now feels increasingly convoluted. The financial district feels the ripple effects of this shift, currency conversions become more complex and the price of goods rises as trade is no longer anchored to the familiar greenback. Companies, now forced to navigate new trading standards, begin to adapt, but the process is far from seamless. Some nations, particularly in the Global South, welcome the new options, while others struggle with the growing pains of a more fragmented system.

In the wake of the USD's decline, a new focus emerges on economic self-sufficiency. Countries, once reliant on the USD for international trade, are now turning inward, building up their industries and reducing their exposure to the fluctuations of global markets. The reliance on global supply chains begins to weaken, replaced by a push toward domestic production in key sectors such as agriculture, energy and technology. Nations start to look less toward the USD and more toward strengthening their own economies, with some of them opting to build up their own currencies.

This shift is not without consequences. The power that the U.S. once held through its control over the USD and, by extension, international sanctions, is beginning to erode. As more countries abandon the greenback in favour of the RMB or other alternatives, the U.S. finds itself with diminished international leverage. Sanctions that once carried the weight of the world no longer hold the same weight. Countries that once feared U.S. financial restrictions now find it easier to bypass them, making it harder for the U.S. to use its economic might to enforce its will.

With the financial system fragmenting, the world begins to experience new tensions. The quiet undercurrents of competition between nations escalate into open discussion about securing economic interests outside of the U.S.-dominated system. Bilateral agreements between countries flourish, as do new regional coalitions that aim to reduce reliance on the U.S. Dollar. The rise of regional economic blocs is inevitable. Countries align themselves with those that share economic or political interests. But with this rise in new economic groupings, particularly from BRICS, comes the risk of deeper geopolitical conflict.

China, now the linchpin of the new financial order, pushes further to assert its dominance. The BRICS coalition expands its influence, challenging the U.S. and its allies. The G7, long accustomed to dictating global financial rules, watches warily as the balance of power begins to shift. With China's rise, there is both an opportunity and a challenge— opportunity for countries seeking alternatives to U.S. dominance, but also a growing rivalry with the West that could spark more than just economic disputes. [See Study Notes 6]

As the fragmentation continues, the USD slowly loses its central place in the global economy. Multiple settlement systems take root, creating a patchwork of financial arrangements that complicate trade and economic cooperation. The world, once comfortably integrated into a single reserve currency system, now faces a more complicated and uncertain future.

Global integration begins to fragment as countries turn to their own currencies, forge their own economic alliances and set their own trading standards. The absence of a common financial language brings with it a new set of challenges, higher transaction costs, more volatile markets and a loss of the unified system that had allowed global trade to flourish for so long.

In this world, cooperation becomes more critical than ever. Without a single financial anchor, nations must navigate a more complicated web of relationships, with power shifting to those who can build alliances and manage their own currencies effectively. The U.S. and other Western powers must learn to adapt to a new, multipolar world, one where the USD no longer reigns supreme and the future of global finance is uncertain.

RMB SUCCEEDS USD SCENARIO
Fast forward, in 2030 (*hypothetically*), the global economic landscape begins to shift in ways that no one had anticipated just a decade ago. At first, the signs are subtle as countries slowly starting to settle their trade agreements in Chinese Renminbi (RMB) rather than U.S. Dollars. But over the next few years, this trickle becomes a flood. A new, unspoken reality begins to take hold: the USD is no longer the undisputed global currency. The RMB, is quietly, but undeniably, taking its place.

It begins in Asia. China's Cross-Border Interbank Payment System (CIPS), which had been growing steadily for years, gains more traction. Neighbouring countries that had long traded with China start to favour the RMB for cross-border transactions, gradually distancing themselves from the USD. A few years later, even countries in Africa, Latin America and the Middle East follow suit, realising that transacting in RMB is not only more practical but also beneficial to their own economies. The RMB, once viewed with scepticism on the global stage, is now the preferred currency for international trade.

The change is seamless for some, but for others, it's a jarring experience. Global financial institutions begin to shift their operations, transitioning from the old USD-based trading standards to a new framework centered around the RMB. Banks once deeply embedded in the USD system now find themselves restructuring their portfolios and trading systems. The once dominant U.S. Dollar is relegated to a secondary position as China's influence grows ever stronger.

Nations that had long aligned themselves with the U.S. in a USD-centric world now find themselves at a crossroads. Some embrace the change. Countries in Asia, already closely tied to China's economic web, rush to deepen their ties, eager to reap the rewards of being part of China's rising sphere of influence. The ASEAN countries, once hesitant to move away from the USD, find themselves drawn into China's orbit, aligning their financial systems with the RMB to secure long-term growth.

Others, however, resist. Europe, for example, still clings to the legacy of the U.S.-dominated global order, hesitant to fully relinquish its reliance on the U.S. Dollar. The European Union, while supportive of closer economic ties with China, sees the shift to the RMB as a threat to its long-standing influence in the global financial system. The geopolitical tension that arises between the East and the West grows palpable. Some European nations call for a counterbalance, a new financial framework, perhaps led by the EUR, to rival China's burgeoning dominance.

Meanwhile, in Washington, the realisation begins to settle in: the U.S. is no longer the unquestioned leader of the global financial system. The political fallout is immediate. With the USD's decline, so too does the U.S.'s leverage over global trade. Economic sanctions, once a powerful tool for U.S. foreign policy, lose their effectiveness. Countries once fearful of U.S. retaliation now find themselves emboldened, free to pursue their own economic interests without the looming threat of USD-based penalties. This shift leads to a fragmentation of the international financial system.

As more countries adopt the RMB for international trade, the effects ripple through global markets. At first, it's small and almost unnoticeable; commodities like oil and gold are traded more frequently in RMB. But then, in 2035, China announces a bold move: the RMB is now a reserve currency, replacing the U.S. Dollar as the cornerstone of global finance. Major global institutions, like the International Monetary Fund (IMF) and the World Bank, begin to adjust their frameworks to account for the new reality. Central banks around the world begin to stockpile RMB, creating a new international monetary order that is unrecognisable from the previous USD-dominated system.

For China, this shift has been years in the making. Its strategy has been one of patience, working quietly in the background while the world watched the United States wane, distracted by its own internal struggles and geopolitical tensions. Like Edmond Dantès in *The Count of Monte Cristo*, China bided its time, waiting for the right moment to emerge. Now, with the RMB firmly entrenched as the world's reserve currency, China takes centre stage in global economic diplomacy. It is no longer just an economic powerhouse; it is the global financial leader and the world's most influential superpower.

Yet, with this power comes significant responsibility. As the RMB becomes the cornerstone of international trade, China finds itself navigating a delicate balancing act. It must manage its own internal economic stability while ensuring that no rival power emerges to challenge its leadership. As more nations align themselves with the Chinese-led economic order, the political dynamics between East and West grow more complex. The U.S., now struggling to maintain its influence, attempts to reassert its power in other ways; through military strength, trade deals and diplomatic manoeuvres. But it's clear that the world is no longer as it was before.

By 2040, the global financial system is a vastly different place. The USD, once the dominant currency in every corner of the world, is now just one of many currencies vying for attention. The RMB, however, has emerged not only as a global currency but as the anchor of a new multipolar world order. China's growing influence is felt not just in the global economy, but in the political and diplomatic spheres as well.

This new world is marked by increased competition, both in economic and geopolitical terms. Nations that had once operated under the umbrella of the U.S. Dollar-based system must now navigate a complex web of economic partnerships and rivalries. The U.S. is no longer the sole superpower but part of a new, more balanced global landscape.

The shift from the USD to the RMB has reshaped the world as we know it. The transition was not without its challenges, but for China, it was the culmination of decades of careful planning and strategy. As the world moves into this new era, the balance of power is in flux. The stage is set for a more dynamic, multipolar world; one where the influence of the U.S. has waned and China stands at the centre of global finance.

USD REMAINS IN INTENSIVE CARE SCENARIO

This scenario unfolds before us as the world watches the U.S. Dollar (USD) cling to its position as the dominant global reserve currency. The room is filled with tension as critical decisions are made on the future of the USD and its place in the international financial system. If the U.S. manages to navigate its structural challenges and restore confidence in its economic leadership, the world could remain anchored to the familiar power of the USD. But the path is far from certain.

The U.S. government knows that it cannot continue its current trajectory. The fiscal debt and the twin deficits, in both the fiscal and the current account, loom over the nation like dark clouds threatening to burst. But there's hope. A long-term commitment to fiscal discipline could be the key to stabilising the U.S. economy and maintaining the USD's role at the heart of global trade. The country must reduce public debt and find a way to balance its finances without leaning too heavily on excessive borrowing. It's a daunting task, but not an impossible one.

Behind closed doors, policymakers discuss the need for prudent public spending. Infrastructure, technology and growth-oriented investments must take precedence over wasteful expenditures. The message is clear: the world needs to see that the U.S. is not only capable of managing its finances but is committed to long-term economic stability. Only then will global markets remain confident in the USD. Years after assuming office, imagine Donald Trump's and Elon Musk's Department of Government Efficiency *(DOGE)* living up to post-election hype. They have been making good progress to reduce the fiscal deficit albeit as a pace slower than their own expectations because they realise that rolling back years of social programs and military spending will take time. U.S. fiscal debt exceeds $40 Trillion towards the end of Trump's presidential tour of duty which works out to be an approximate burden of $120,000 per American.

But there is another factor that could make or break the U.S. Dollar's future; the relationship with China. The tension between the two global superpowers has been palpable, but perhaps a shift is coming. Trade wars, tariffs and geopolitical rivalry have strained the global economy for years. However, what if, in an unexpected turn, the U.S. and China decide to work together, resolve key trade issues and embrace a more cooperative relationship? The possibility of a thaw in relations could provide the stability the global economy desperately needs.

In Washington, the debate rages on: can the U.S. restore its credibility on the world stage? The country must show consistent, responsible leadership, engage diplomatically with key global players and manage international conflicts with skill. Only then can it maintain the trust required to sustain the USD as the world's reserve currency.

But the future remains uncertain. As the U.S. works to restore balance and confidence, the world watches closely, waiting to see if these objectives can truly be realised. Will the U.S. rise to the challenge, or will political and economic realities conspire to drag the nation back into the chaos of fiscal mismanagement?

On the other hand, the USD may hold on to its place as the global reserve currency, but at what cost? Without addressing these looming issues, the U.S. risks a stagnant future. Persistent fiscal deficits and political gridlock could erode confidence in the USD. The global financial system, reliant on an increasingly fragile U.S. economy, could face prolonged inefficiency. The "USD Elephant" would continue to dominate, blocking progress and stifling innovation. Digital currencies, CBDCs, and other alternatives may never truly take root if the global financial system remains shackled to an outdated currency system.

Meanwhile, the possibility of a "one-time" depreciation of the USD looms. It could come suddenly, like the silent Plaza Accord of the 1980s, leaving the world to deal with the fallout. The risk of a sharp devaluation could prompt a series of painful adjustments in the global financial system. Lenders may no longer be willing to accept the USD on existing terms, and the currency could find itself in a spiral of decline.

The future of the U.S. Dollar is far from guaranteed. The outcome hinges on whether the U.S. can adapt to the changing global landscape, reform its fiscal policies and take the lead responsibly on the world stage. If the nation fails to meet these challenges, the world may remain stuck with the USD Elephant in the room, an outdated and increasingly irrelevant global currency that blocks progress and impedes the potential for a new, more efficient economic order. The global financial system, already teetering on the edge, could be forced into a new phase of instability and change.

COLLATERAL DAMAGE

The stage is set for a dramatic shift in the world's economic structure that will reverberate across the globe. As the U.S. Dollar (USD) loses its place as the world's reserve currency, the ripples of change spread far and wide, touching every nation. The question now is not if this will happen, but how it will unfold, and that will determine the scale of the chaos or opportunity for countries around the world.

A gradual decline in the USD's status would provide some relief, but the adjustment would still be challenging. Countries that have long depended on the USD especially those heavily dollarised, would find themselves with time to adapt. Slowly but surely, they could pivot to other currencies, diversify their reserves and adjust their policies to cope with the loss of the USD's dominance. Emerging markets, in particular, would be hit, but a more gradual transition might offer them a fighting chance. However, if the

USD were to collapse suddenly, perhaps through an abrupt move to a new reserve currency or a sudden depreciation, then the consequences would be severe and swift. The shockwaves would first slam into developing nations, their fragile economies devastated by the sudden loss of value and purchasing power.

In this chaotic scenario, the U.S. would find itself in uncharted territory. The immediate consequence of losing the USD's reserve status would likely be a sharp depreciation of the currency. The U.S. Dollar, once seen as a rock-solid pillar of the global economy, would lose its sheen. For U.S. consumers, the impact would be felt immediately; inflation would surge and the purchasing power of American households would be decimated. The cost of living would skyrocket and social unrest could follow as everyday people bear the brunt of economic hardship.

To combat the rampant inflation, the Federal Reserve might be forced into action, hiking interest rates to stem the tide of devaluation. However, this would not come without its own challenges. Borrowing costs would rise, affecting the U.S. government, businesses and consumers alike. The pain would extend far beyond American borders, as emerging markets, many of which carry debt denominated in USD would see their own borrowing costs surge. In an already fragile financial environment, this could lead to defaults, bankruptcies and potential financial crises in countries unable to manage their increased debt burdens.

For those nations that have dollarised their economies, countries that have adopted the USD as their primary currency, an immediate fallout would be unavoidable. These economies, tied directly to the fate of the USD, would find themselves in freefall. Without a dominant global currency to anchor their systems, hyperinflation could take root as these nations' currencies lose value in the wake of the USD's collapse. The financial sector would crumble, consumer purchasing power would evaporate and social upheaval could quickly follow. In some cases, nations may be forced to abandon their pegged exchange rates, switching to alternative currencies such as the Chinese RMB or the EUR, or even adopting a basket of currencies. This would only introduce further instability, as currency shifts bring added volatility to an already unpredictable global market.

The repercussions would not be confined to the U.S. and its immediate partners. The world economy would feel the effects as well. As the USD weakens, so too does global trade. Import costs would rise for both the U.S. and its trading partners, leading to inflationary pressures worldwide. Emerging markets, already vulnerable, would feel the impact most acutely, as they would be disproportionately affected by rising costs and the disruption of global supply chains. Nations dependent on U.S. exports would scale back purchases, sending shockwaves through the global economy. A sharp decline in U.S. exports could potentially trigger a global recession, one that would spiral as other nations struggled to cope with the shock.

Emerging markets, especially those already on the economic precipice, would face a crisis of their own. Debt burdens would become insurmountable as borrowing costs soar, and the weak USD exacerbates inflation. Defaults become more common and austerity measures would follow as governments scramble to manage the crisis. The poor and vulnerable would be hit hardest, their already fragile economic positions worsened by the storm of rising prices and shrinking opportunities.

At the same time, the global economic order could fracture into a more fragmented, regionalised system. Countries might shift focus to self-sufficiency or forge new regional trade agreements to protect their own interests. Instead of a unified global system, the world could splinter into competing blocs, each pursuing its own economic interests. This would lead to greater fragmentation, as nations turn inward to safeguard their economies, reducing the level of international cooperation that has defined the global economic system for decades.

The shift from a unipolar global order, with the U.S. at the helm, to a more fragmented and polarised world, would not be without its dangers. As the USD fades without a clear successor, global cooperation could collapse under the weight of regionalism and protectionism. The absence of a dominant global currency would make it harder for nations to collaborate on pressing issues like climate change, pandemics or international conflicts. In the worst-case scenario, the world could descend into a period of economic isolationism, marked by rising nationalism and a breakdown of the interconnected global system that has underpinned growth and stability for decades.

As the U.S. Dollar slips into history, the world faces an uncertain future. Whether the transition to a new reserve currency happens gradually or suddenly, the consequences are undeniable. Emerging markets will bear the brunt of the pain and the global economy may become more fragmented and polarised. The U.S. will lose its ability to shape global policy and the global stage will enter a new, more uncertain chapter. The USD's departure could mark the end of the post-war economic order, leaving in its wake a world struggling to adjust to a new and uncharted economic landscape.

WISHFUL THINKING: THE SEMI-FIAT RESERVE CURRENCY

The idea of a semi-fiat currency partially backed by gold and silver is an intriguing one, offering a potential middle ground between the flexibility of fiat money and the stability of commodity-backed currencies. While largely speculative, this *"wishful thinking"* currency could address some of the fundamental issues of both the fiat system, like the USD, and the commodity-backed system, like the gold standard. However, the proposal comes with its own set of advantages and challenges that need careful consideration.

HISTORICAL CONTEXT

The concept of a supranational currency is not novel. John Maynard Keynes, during the Bretton Woods Conference in 1944, proposed the creation of the "Bancor," a global currency that would be backed by a basket of commodities. The idea was to address the inherent risks and instability of relying on a single currency like the USD, which was prone to the economic fluctuations of the issuing country. Despite its rejection, Keynes' idea of a global currency found some life in the form of Special Drawing Rights (SDRs) introduced by the International Monetary Fund (IMF). SDRs, although not a currency per se, serve as a synthetic reserve asset based on a basket of major currencies, including the Chinese RMB. Yet, both the Bancor and SDRs have only partially addressed the problem, as they still rely on fiat currencies, which lack a tangible anchor like gold or silver, assets that have historically provided a more stable store of value.

PLUSES OF A SEMI-FIAT CURRENCY

A semi-fiat currency, backed partially by tangible assets like gold or silver, could offer several advantages over fully fiat systems:

- **Stability and Confidence**: Tying part of the currency's value to physical assets provides a degree of stability. Unlike pure fiat money, which depends on governmental policies and economic performance, a semi-fiat currency has an intrinsic value derived from gold or silver. This backing could bolster confidence, particularly in times of economic turbulence or inflation.
- **Hedge Against Inflation**: Gold and silver have proven to be resilient during periods of inflation. A currency backed by these precious metals could function as a hedge, offering protection when fiat currencies devalue. A global shift to such a currency could help stabilise international trade by reducing volatility typically associated with fiat money fluctuations.
- **Attracting Broader Adoption**: Countries holding significant reserves of gold or silver might be more inclined to adopt a currency that is partially backed by these metals. In regions where economies are looking for alternatives to the USD, a semi-fiat currency could hold greater appeal, especially among emerging economies that are seeking more stability and independence from the fluctuations of U.S. fiscal and monetary policy.

MINUSES OF A SEMI-FIAT CURRENCY

However, several challenges would accompany the adoption of a semi-fiat currency:

- **Limits on Central Bank Flexibility**: A semi-fiat currency would limit central banks' ability to engage in expansive monetary policies. With part of the value tied to finite resources like gold and silver, central banks would have less room to manoeuvre when economic conditions require rapid action, such as lowering interest rates or undertaking quantitative easing. This could hinder the ability of central banks to respond to crises or stimulate growth.
- **Gold and Silver Supply Constraints**: The amount of gold and silver required to back such a currency could pose significant challenges. As demand for the currency grows, the need for precious metals would rise, potentially driving up their prices and creating volatility in the market. Countries would also face geopolitical challenges in securing and accumulating enough physical reserves of these metals, possibly leading to conflicts or tensions over access to these valuable resources.
- **Geopolitical and Trade Barriers**: Achieving widespread international acceptance of a semi-fiat currency would not be easy. Many countries might be reluctant to shift away from established fiat currencies, especially the USD. If the new currency were dominated by one or a few countries, this could create geopolitical friction, especially if the backing nation was perceived as exerting too much control over the global monetary system. Additionally, maintaining transparency and trust in the system would be challenging, as countries would need to ensure that the backing assets were securely held and properly managed.

RMB and EUR as Semi-Fiat Candidates

Two currencies, the RMB and EUR, stand out as potential candidates for transformation into semi-fiat reserve currencies:

- **RMB**: China has been positioning the RMB as a global reserve currency, with Beijing building substantial gold reserves to hedge against USD dependency. However, the RMB faces significant obstacles in achieving full global adoption, including capital controls, lack of full currency convertibility, and concerns over transparency and governance in China. A partially gold-backed RMB could address some of these concerns, but for widespread adoption, China would need to liberalise its financial markets, increase political transparency and ensure the stability of its currency.
- **EUR**: The Euro already serves as one of the world's leading reserve currencies, backed by the European Central Bank (ECB) and the economic strength of the Eurozone. A semi-fiat euro, partially backed by gold and silver, could make it a more appealing alternative to the USD, particularly for countries seeking to reduce their exposure to U.S. economic volatility. However, the diverse economic conditions within the Eurozone pose a challenge for the ECB. The flexibility needed to manage crises in specific member states might be restricted by the gold-backed structure, creating tensions between maintaining currency stability and addressing the economic needs of individual member states.

Benefits of Multiple Semi-Fiat Reserve Currencies

The adoption of multiple semi-fiat currencies, such as the RMB and EUR, would offer several benefits:
- **Diversification of Risks**: Countries could diversify their exposure to the risks of a single reserve currency, like the USD, by choosing between the RMB and EUR or other semi-fiat currencies. This would reduce vulnerability to fluctuations in the value of one currency and provide greater stability.
- **Greater Global Economic Integration**: A multi-currency system involving semi-fiat currencies could enhance global economic integration. A diversified basket of reserve currencies would make it easier for countries to collaborate on trade, investment and international policy, reducing reliance on the dominance of any one currency.
- **Encouraging U.S. Participation**: If the RMB and EUR successfully transformed into semi-fiat currencies, the U.S. might reconsider its own approach to the USD. This could encourage the U.S. to resolve its fiscal challenges and potentially introduce a semi-gold-backed USD, thereby reasserting its leadership in the global financial system.

Complementary Roles of Payment Platforms and Cryptocurrencies

In this evolving financial ecosystem, payment platforms and cryptocurrencies could complement semi-fiat reserve currencies:
- **Seamless Exchange Between Fiat and Digital Assets**: Payment platforms like PayPal that support cryptocurrency transactions could bridge the gap between traditional fiat currencies and digital assets. The integration of blockchain technology with existing financial systems allows for greater transaction efficiency, improved financial inclusion *(easy access to digital accounts to transact without having to open a bank account)* and the ability to handle multi-currency transactions without undermining the stability of traditional reserve currencies.
- **Enhancing Utility of Semi-Fiat Currencies**: Rather than replacing traditional currencies, cryptocurrencies and payment platforms could enhance the functionality of semi-fiat reserve currencies. By integrating blockchain-based systems into global trade, they could streamline international payments and reduce

the reliance on a single currency, while still allowing semi-fiat currencies to function effectively within the global financial system.

In conclusion, while the vision of a global semi-fiat currency system is idealistic, it is not beyond the realm of possibility. A currency backed partially by tangible assets like gold and silver could offer greater stability, act as a hedge against inflation and help resolve some of the vulnerabilities inherent in fiat currency systems. However, substantial challenges, ranging from gold and silver supply constraints to geopolitical resistance, would need to be overcome. By complementing these semi-fiat currencies with advanced payment platforms and cryptocurrencies, a more integrated and stable global financial ecosystem could emerge, though it would likely evolve gradually. As nations search for alternatives to the USD, the concept of a multi-currency system backed by precious metals might become more feasible, marking a potential new era in global economic governance.

FINAL CONCLUSION FOR NOW

The potential loss of the USD as the world's reserve currency would undoubtedly trigger a period of economic instability, with profound implications for global trade, finance and geopolitical alliances. If this occurs, nations will need to navigate the shifting landscape by diversifying their reserves, forming regional trade partnerships and exploring alternative currencies to mitigate the risks associated with the decline of USD dominance. The shift from the USD to another currency, like the RMB, would not be a simple transition. It would require countries to reassess their engagement with China, especially across the three core pillars of Politics, Economics and Military (PoEM).

Such a transition would push nations to rethink their financial strategies and strengthen their resilience. Many institutions, both public and private, would find their preparedness severely tested. The missteps of institutions like Long-Term Capital Management (LTCM), Silicon Valley Bank (SVB) and Lehman Brothers serve as cautionary tales of how complacency and lack of risk mitigation can lead to catastrophic consequences.

The decline of the USD, though complex and gradual, is a challenge that countries are already facing. Strategic preparation is essential for ensuring resilience in the event of a global shift away from the USD. Rather than fearing the future, nations must focus on understanding the risks involved and plan accordingly. As Marie Curie wisely said, *"Nothing in life is to be feared, it is only to be understood. Now is the time to understand more, so that we may fear less."*

This idea of understanding the forces behind the potential decline of the USD should inspire readers to continue exploring the subject, developing solutions and preparing for the future. The ideas in this book are just the beginning of what could be a long and complex journey.

In the end, just like in *The Count of Monte Cristo*, where the protagonist ended with two words **"Wait and Hope"** the conclusion for the USD and its global dominance could very well come down to: **"Prepare and Act."**

REFERENCES
Chapter 1
1. Thaler, Britannica: https://www.britannica.com/topic/thaler
2. Gross, Samatha, *"Reducing US Oil demand, not production, is the way forward for Climate"*, Brookings Institution, Sep 2023.
https://www.brookings.edu/articles/reducing-us-oil-demand-not-production-is-the-way-forward-for-the-climate/
3. Gold Price, *"Gold Demand Trends Q1 2024"*, World Gold Council, Apr 30, 2023.
https://www.gold.org/goldhub/research/gold-demand-trends/gold-demand-trends-q1-2024
4. Hunt, Paul-Alain, *"Iron ore majors ramp up supply even as China faces challenges"*, Mining.com, Jul 17, 2024.
https://www.mining.com/web/iron-ore-majors-ramp-up-supply-even-as-china-faces-challenges/
5. Gelber, G. Harry, *"China as "Victim"? The Opium War That Wasn't"*, Publisher: Minda de Gunzburg, Centre for European Studies, Harvard University, 2006.
https://www.thecrimson.com/article/2006/2/23/the-opium-war-that-wasnt-one/
6. *"Box 1.4. Did the Plaza Accord Cause Japan's Lost Decades?"*, International Monetary Fund, Apr 2011.
https://www.imf.org/-/media/Websites/IMF/imported-flagship-issues/external/pubs/ft/weo/2011/01/c1/_box14pdf.ashx
7. Office of the Historian, *"Rapprochement with China, 1972"*.
https://history.state.gov/milestones/1969-1976/rapprochement-china
8. U.S. GDP Data, *"U.S. National GDP and Personal Income"*, U.S. Bureau of Economic Analysis, Oct 14, 2024.
https://www.bea.gov/itable/national-gdp-and-personal-income
9. Andrew Chatzky, James McBride and Mohammed Aly Sergie, *"NAFTA and the USMCA: Weighing the Impact of North American Trade"*, Council on Foreign Relations, Jul 1, 2020.
https://www.cfr.org/backgrounder/naftas-economic-impact#chapter-title-0-2
10. Atomic Bomb, *"Decision to Drop the Atomic Bomb"*, Harry S. Truman Library & Museum.
https://www.trumanlibrary.gov/education/presidential-inquiries/decision-drop-atomic-bomb
11. IMF, *"The Asian Crisis; Causes and Cures"*, International Monetary Fund, Jun 1998.
https://www.imf.org/external/pubs/ft/fandd/1998/06/imfstaff.htm
12. Auer, Raphael and Boehmer, Rainer, *"Central bank digital currency: the quest for minimally invasive technology"*, Bank for International Settlements (BIS), Jun 2021.
https://www.bis.org/publ/work948.htm

Chapter 2
1. Steam Locomotive, *"Inventions of the Industrial Revolution"*, Britannica.
https://www.britannica.com/list/inventors-and-inventions-of-the-industrial-revolution
2. Electric Generators and Motors, *"Inventions of the Industrial Revolution"*, Britannica.
https://www.britannica.com/list/inventors-and-inventions-of-the-industrial-revolution
3. Telegraph and Telephone, *"Inventions of the Industrial Revolution"*, Britannica.
https://www.britannica.com/list/inventors-and-inventions-of-the-industrial-revolution
4. Victoria, *"The Battle of Trafalgar"*, National Maritime Museum, Greenwich, London.
https://www.rmg.co.uk/stories/topics/battle-of-trafalgar
5. Treaty of Versailles, *"The Paris Peace Conference and the Treaty of Versailles"*, Office of the Historian. https://history.state.gov/milestones/1914-1920/paris-peace
6. Second World War, National Army Museum UK.
https://www.nam.ac.uk/explore/second-world-war
7. Bretton Woods, *"Creation of the Bretton Woods System"*, Federal Reserve History.
https://www.federalreservehistory.org/essays/bretton-woods-created
8. Triffin Dilemma, *"Nixon Ends Convertibility of U.S. Dollars to Gold and Announces Wage/Price Controls"*, Federal Reserve History, Nov 22, 2013.
https://www.federalreservehistory.org/essays/gold-convertibility-ends
9. End of Bretton Woods, *"Launch of the Bretton Woods System"*, Federal Reserve History.
https://www.federalreservehistory.org/essays/bretton-woods-launched
10. Hall, Jason, *"What is Fiat Currency"*, The Motley Fool, Aug 16, 2024.
https://www.fool.com/terms/f/fiat-currency/
11. Historical Exchange Rates, International Monetary Fund IMF.
https://www.imf.org/en/Home

Chapter 3
1. OPEC, *"Oil and Gas Industry: A Research Guide"*, Library of Congress.
   https://guides.loc.gov/oil-and-gas-industry/organizations
2. Auto Price Fixing, *"Nine Automobile Parts Manufacturers and Two Executives Agree to Plead Guilty to Fixing Prices on Automobile Parts Sold to U.S. Car Manufacturers and Installed in U.S. Cars"*, Office of Public Affairs, U.S. Department of Justice, Sep 26, 2013.
   https://www.justice.gov/opa/pr/nine-automobile-parts-manufacturers-and-two-executives-agree-to-plead-guilty-fixing-prices
3. Microsoft, *"U.S. V. Microsoft: Court's Findings Of Fact"*, AntiTrust Division, U.S. Department of Justice, Nov 1999. https://www.justice.gov/atr/us-v-microsoft-courts-findings-fact
4. Swindle, Orson, *"What Are We Learning from the Microsoft Case?"*, Federal Trade Commission, Sep 30, 1999.
   https://www.ftc.gov/news-events/news/speeches/what-are-we-learning-microsoft-case
5. Barkin, Noah, *"The EU and Its EV Duties"*, German Marshall Fund, Sep 16, 2024.
   https://www.gmfus.org/news/eu-and-its-ev-duties
6. Venon, Dan, *"Orange Juice Market Manipulation (1989) – The Full Story Unveiled"*, Shipping and Commodity Academy, Mar 21, 2024.
   https://shippingandcommodityacademy.com/blog/orange-juice-market-manipulation-1989-the-full-story-unveiled/
7. HKD Peg, *"Milestones of Monetary Reform"*, Hong Kong Monetary Authority.
   https://www.hkma.gov.hk/eng/key-functions/money/linked-exchange-rate-system/milestones-of-monetary-reform/
8. Ukraine-Russia War, *"EU Sanctions against Russia"*, European Council;
   https://www.consilium.europa.eu/en/policies/sanctions-against-russia/
9. Blinova Ekaterina, *"Why Anti-Russia Sanctions are Self-Inflicted Disaster for US & EU"*, Mar 1 2022.
   https://www.khmertimeskh.com/501033426/why-anti-russia-sanctions-are-self-inflicted-disaster-for-us-eu/
10. Leung, Christine, *"10 Examples of Trade Embargoes"*, The Borgen Project, Jul 23, 2018.
    https://borgenproject.org/examples-of-trade-embargoes/
11. Mirandette, John, "U.S. Sanctions and Venezuela's Poor", The Borgen Project, Sep 11, 2017.
    https://borgenproject.org/sanctions-and-venezuelas-poor/
12. WTO, *"The WTO at Twenty: Challenges and Achievements"*, World Trade Organisation, published in 2015. https://www.wto.org/english/res_e/publications_e/wto_at_twenty_e.htm
13. China Brief Team, *"US-China Relations in the Biden Era: A Timeline"*, China Briefing, Nov 1, 2024.
    https://www.china-briefing.com/news/us-china-relations-in-the-biden-era-a-timeline/

Chapter 4
1. 1893 Depression, *"Banking Panics of the Gilded Age 1863-1913"*, Federal Reserve History, Dec 4, 2015. https://www.federalreservehistory.org/essays/banking-panics-of-the-gilded-age
2. Medicare and Medicaid, *"Medicare and Medicaid Act 1965"*, National Archives U.S.
   https://www.archives.gov/milestone-documents/medicare-and-medicaid-act
3. 1929 Depression, *"The Great Depression - 1929"*, National Archives U.S.
   https://hoover.archives.gov/exhibits/great-depression
4. Cleveland, Harlan, *"The Cold War"*; The National Archives and Record Administration, Oct 21 2006.
   https://www.archives.gov/research/foreign-policy/cold-war/symposium/cleveland.html
5. Oil Embargo, *"Oil Embargo 1973-1974"*, Office of the Historian,
   https://history.state.gov/milestones/1969-1976/oil-embargo
6. Gascon S. Charles and Karson Gavin, *"Growth in Tech Sector Returns to Glory Days of the 1990s"*, Federal Reserve Bank of St Louis, Jul 25, 2017.
   https://www.stlouisfed.org/publications/regional-economist/second-quarter-2017/growth-in-tech-sector-returns-to-glory-days-of-the-1990s
7. Duca V. John, *"Subprime Mortgage Crisis 2007–2010"*, Federal Reserve Bank of Dallas, Nov 22, 2013. https://www.federalreservehistory.org/essays/subprime-mortgage-crisis
8. Turner John, *"Why did the global financial crisis of 2007-09 happen?"*, Banks & Financial Markets Economics Observatory, Sep 4, 2023.
   https://www.economicsobservatory.com/why-did-the-global-financial-crisis-of-2007-09-happen
9. QE Rounds, *"Large Scale Asset Purchases"*, Federal Reserve Bank of New York.
   https://www.newyorkfed.org/markets/programs-archive/large-scale-asset-purchases

10. SVB, *"Review of the Federal Reserve's Supervision and Regulation of Silicon Valley Bank"*, Federal Reserve, Apr 2023.
https://www.federalreserve.gov/publications/2023-April-SVB-Evolution-of-Silicon-Valley-Bank.htm
11. Coughlin, Cletus, Pakko R Michael, Poole William, *"How Dangerous Is the U.S. Current Account Deficit?"*, Federal Reserve Bank of St Louis, Apr 1, 2006.
https://www.stlouisfed.org/publications/regional-economist/april-2006/how-dangerous-is-the-us-current-account-deficit
12. U.S. Federal Debt, U.S. Department of Treasury, Fiscal Service
13. Ross, Jean, *"The Tax Cuts and Job Act Failed to Deliver Promised Benefits"*, Center for American Progress, Apr 30, 2024. https://www.americanprogress.org/article/the-tax-cuts-and-jobs-act-failed-to-deliver-promised-benefits/
14. CARES Act, *"What's in the CARES Act? Here's a Summary,"* Peter G. Peterson Foundation, Apr 22, 2020. https://www.pgpf.org/infographic/whats-in-the-cares-act-heres-a-summary
15. Ihrig, Jane and Wolla A. Scott, *"The Fed, How Does the Fed Use Its Monetary Policy Tools to Influence the Economy?"*, Federal Reserve Bank of St Louis, May 2, 2022.
https://www.stlouisfed.org/publications/page-one-economics/2022/05/02/how-does-the-fed-use-its-monetary-policy-tools-to-influence-the-economy

Chapter 5
1. ARRA 2009, *"The Economic Impact of the American Recovery and Reinvestment Act of 2009 First Quarterly Report"*, the White House President Barak Obama;
https://obamawhitehouse.archives.gov/administration/eop/cea/Economic-Impact/
2. Dodd Frank Act 2010, *"Wall Street Reform: The Dodd Frank Act"*, the White House President Barak Obama; https://obamawhitehouse.archives.gov/economy/middle-class/dodd-frank-wall-street-reform
3. Oshagbemi Comfort and Sheiner Louise, *"Which Provisions of the Tax Cuts and Jobs Act expire in 2025?"*, Brookings Institute, Sep 5, 2024. https://www.brookings.edu/articles/which-provisions-of-the-tax-cuts-and-jobs-act-expire-in-2025/
4. ARPA and CARES Acts, *"ARPA vs. CARES: What's the Difference?"*, MCCi;
https://mccinnovations.com/insights/blog/arpa-vs-cares-act-what-is-the-difference/
5. Wei, Maggie, *"China's currency rises in cross-border trade but remains limited globally"*, Goldman Sachs. Jul 26, 2023.
https://www.goldmansachs.com/insights/articles/chinas-currency-rises-in-cross-border-trade-but-remains-limited-globally

Chapter 6
1. Chang, Sea-Jin, *"The Rise of the Chaebols"*, Cambridge University Press, published 2003. Pg 3 to 16.
2. Shirreff, David, *"Lessons from the collapse of hedge fuds, long term capital management"*, Econometrics Laboratory, eml.berkeley.edu.
https://eml.berkeley.edu/~webfac/craine/e137_f03/137lessons.pdf
3. Antoncic, Madelyn, *"Not Too Big To Fail: Why Lehman Had to Go Bankrupt"*, Knowledge at Wharton Podcast, Sep 28, 2018.
https://knowledge.wharton.upenn.edu/podcast/knowledge-at-wharton-podcast/the-good-reasons-why-lehman-failed/
4. Hetler, Amanda, *"Silicon Valley Bank collapse explained: What you need to know"*, Mar 13, 2024.
https://www.techtarget.com/whatis/feature/Silicon-Valley-Bank-collapse-explained-What-you-need-to-know
5. Kato, Hironori, *"Norinchukin Bank's losses expected to grow to 1.5 trillion yen"*, Asahi Shimbun, Jun19, 2024. https://www.asahi.com/ajw/articles/15311096
6. RMS Titanic Fact, *National Maritime Museum, Greenwich, London.*
,https://www.rmg.co.uk/stories/topics/rms-titanic-facts#:~:text=The%20Titanic%20had%20a%20swimming%20pool%20on%20board&text=In%20first%20class%20there%20were,than%20those%20on%20other%20liners.
7. Amaranth https://www.investopedia.com/articles/mutualfund/05/hedgefundfailure.asp
8. McDowell, Hayley, *"The Collapse of Archegos Capital Management"*, thetradenews.com, Jul 16, 2021. https://www.thetradenews.com/the-collapse-of-archegos-capital-management/
9. Clowes, H Samuel, *"Raj Rajaratnam and Insider Trading"*, Seven Pillars Institute.
https://sevenpillarsinstitute.org/case-studies/raj-rajaratnam-and-insider-trading-2/
10. Brookings Institution, https://www.brookings.edu/about-us/
11. Truitt, Sarah, *"When Margaret Thatcher Crushed a British Miners' Strike"*, History.com, Sep12, 2023.
https://www.history.com/news/margaret-thatcher-miners-strike-iron-lady

12. *"Lee Kuan Yew vs the SIA Strikers"*, May 1, 2015.
    https://www.youtube.com/watch?v=ytMXSLeqFMY
13. Buckle, Mark, *"Black Cat, White Cat…"*, chinadaily.com.cn, Aug 02, 2018,
    https://www.chinadaily.com.cn/a/201808/02/WS5b728ae4a310add14f385b4a.html
14. *"203. Joint Statement Following Discussions With Leaders of the People's Republic of China"*, Office of the Historian, Shanghai, Feb 27, 1972.
    https://history.state.gov/historicaldocuments/frus1969-76v17/d203
15. Field, James, *"KfW bank issues digital bond using 'Trigger Solution"*, coingeek.com, Sep28 2024.
    https://coingeek.com/kfw-bank-issues-digital-bond-using-trigger-solution/

SUGGESTED READING LIST

1. Eichengreen, Barry, *"Global Imbalances and the Lesson of Bretton Woods"*, The MIT Press, published 2010.

2. Eichengreen, Barry, *"Exorbitant Privilege: The Rise and Fall of the Dolla"*, The Oxford University Press, published 2011.

3. Wen Hua Zong Heng, *"A Journal of Contemporary Chinese Thought"*, May 2024 | Vol. 2, No. 1.
   https://thetricontinental.org/wp-content/uploads/2024/05/20240514_WHZH_Vol2No1_EN.pdf

4. Martin, Nik, *"Dedollarization: How the West boosts China's yuan"*, Deutsche Welle (DW);
   https://www.dw.com/en/dedollarization-how-the-west-is-boosting-chinas-yuan/a-70118356

5. *"Asian Development Bank raises growth forecast but warns over trade sanctions"*, The Irish Times,
   https://www.breakingnews.ie/world/asian-development-bank-raises-growth-forecast-but-warns-over-trade-sanctions-1675953.html

6. *"The Changing Role of the USD"*, Brooking Institute
   https://www.brookings.edu/articles/the-changing-role-of-the-us-dollar/

7. Mooradian G. Maxilllan, *"China's Challenge to the International Economic Order"*, Foreign Policy Research Institute, Foreign Policy Research Institute, Jan 18 2024;
   https://www.fpri.org/article/2024/01/chinas-challenge-to-the-international-economic-order/

8. *"Hong Kong and the Opium Wars"*, The National Archives Hong Kong.
   https://www.nationalarchives.gov.uk/education/resources/hong-kong-and-the-opium-wars/

STUDY NOTES

1. **SWIFT - *Society for Worldwide Interbank Financial Telecommunication***
   https://www.swift.com/about-us/history
   SWIFT is a cooperative utility headquartered in Belgium. It started in 1973 from a consortium of 239 banks from 15 countries. SWIFT messaging service went live in 1977 which replaced the old Telex technology that was the common platform in use then. The key aspects of SWIFT system included a messaging platform, a computer system to validate and route messages, and a set of message standards. The standards allow for a collective understanding of the data across linguistic and systems boundaries and to permit the seamless, automated transmission, receipt and processing of communications exchanged between users. SWIFT is now a global financial infrastructure that spans every continent, more than 200 countries and territories, and services more than 11,000 institutions worldwide.

2. **Disentangling from Sterling: Malaysia and the end of the Bretton Woods system 1965-72, Catherine R Schenk, *University of Glasgow***
   https://papers.ssrn.com/sol3/papers.cfm?abstract_id=1076682
   Abstract: A decade after independence, the Malaysian government and central bank were faced with a series of challenges that forced them to develop an independent policy, leading to the end of the historic role of sterling in their international monetary regime. Like some economies today that are faced with accumulated reserves largely comprised of a depreciating currency (now the US$), Malaysia had to disentangle itself from sterling at a time when there were no clear alternatives since gold was scarce, the US$ was weak and Germany, Switzerland and Japan resisted the use of their currencies as national reserves. This paper uses new archival evidence to show that external obstacles as well as some misjudgement meant that this was only achieved in June 1972, 15 years after Merdeka. This process also reveals new evidence about the post-colonial relations between Malaysia and Britain and sheds new light on the neo-colonial interpretation of the first decade of independence.

3. **Japanese Banana Notes: Japanese Occupation, Military Yen: 1942–1945, National Library Board, Singapore**
   https://www.nlb.gov.sg/main/article-detail?cmsuuid=ac36a2e4-5620-4812-9405-e5bd24023213
   When the Japanese occupied Singapore in 1942, they introduced the military yen. The new currency was commonly referred to as "banana money" because the $10 note featured a banana plant. The prewar British currency was still legal tender but was quickly replaced by the new Japanese currency in the open market.
   The initial issue of "banana money" was serially numbered with control letters and safety features such as a watermark and security thread. Subsequently, large quantities of the currency were issued without security features and the serial numbers disappeared from the notes. The military notes were intended for circulation on par with the Straits and Malayan dollar notes, but their value decreased dramatically over time. By 12 August 1945, the exchange rate had dropped to 950 Japanese military dollars for 1 Straits dollar. The Japanese currency was rendered worthless when it was demonetised by the British after they regained control of Malaya in September 1945.

4. **Cold War, The George Orwell Foundation**
   https://www.orwellfoundation.com/the-orwell-foundation/orwell/essays-and-other-works/you-and-the-atom-bomb/
   "You and the Atom Bomb", written by George Orwel, published on *Tribune*, 19 October 1945.
   Such a prolific writer he was, George Orwell widely credited to be the person to introduce the **"Cold War"** term which depicted the political tensions and military rivalry between the United States and Soviet Union. Yet another notable perspective which Orwell put forth following the atomic bombing events which encapsulates how the nuclear age has lulled us into an uneasy state of peace.
   ". . . . it is likelier to put an end to large-scale wars at the cost of prolonging indefinitely a peace that is no peace".

5. **CAMBODIA: Unified QR Code Payment System Launched by Central Bank, HKTDC Research, Aug 1, 2022**
   https://research.hktdc.com/en/article/MTEzMDE3OTg4MA
   The *National Bank of Cambodia* (*NBC*) has introduced a standardised QR code payment system called *KHQR*, launched on 4 July 2022 replacing all QR codes provided by mobile banking apps. *KHQR* is targeted at retail purchases, and only one QR code will be required for receiving payments

using any of the main mobile apps. This includes *Bakong*, a mobile payments and banking platform operating using the country's digital currency.

Currently, *Bakong* has 37 financial institutions as members, and its use has grown rapidly. About 6.8 million transactions valued at US$2.9 billion had been recorded using the app by November 2021, according to a *Nikkei Asia* report. Mobile users can use *KHQR* codes generated by merchants using *Bakong* or other supported apps for making transactions in Cambodian riel or US dollars. In 2021, electronic payment transactions in Cambodia numbered 707 million totalling US$113 billion, according to the *NBC*.

6. **The BRICS Challenge to the G7 Established International Order, Foreign Policy Research Institute, Sep 20, 2024, Maximillan G. Mooradian**
   https://www.fpri.org/article/2024/09/the-brics-challenge-to-the-g7-established-international-order/
   The BRICS (Brazil, Russia, India, China, South Africa, United Arab Emirates, Saudi Arabia, Iran, Ethiopia, and Egypt) organization, led by China, is challenging the rules-based international order of the G7 (Canada, France, Germany, Italy, Japan, the United Kingdom, the European Union, and the United States), led by the United States.

   BRICS is challenging the established international order in three ways. The first is through an independent economic system that will heavily influence the global market. The second is with an artificial intelligence governance framework that would jeopardize privacy, accountability, transparency, and human rights. Third is the military-regional security alignments that could change the balance of power in regions vital to US national security interests.

   If the United States fails to act, BRICS is likely to grow in strength, align foreign policies against US interests, and have the potential to disrupt the global order that has thus far averted major conflicts.

ABOUT THE AUTHOR

B.Y. Leo practiced engineering in the aerospace sector from the late eighties to the early nineties, designing helicopters for five years in Singapore and France.

In 1985, Leo attended Imperial College London, graduating with a degree in Aeronautical Engineering. During his time there, he was awarded the Finsbury Medal for being the top student and the Olav Henrici Medal for Excellence in Mathematics. In 1993, Leo pursued an MBA (Finance with Distinction) at the Wharton School, University of Pennsylvania. While at Wharton, he lectured undergraduates in Operations Management and served as a teaching assistant in Macroeconomics and Derivatives Mathematics.

Leo began his finance career on Wall Street, New York, in 1995, where he structured, risk-managed and traded complex financial derivatives. His career subsequently took him to London, Tokyo, Hong Kong and Singapore, where he expanded his expertise to include structuring financial solutions for corporates and investors across various asset classes, including foreign exchange, fixed income, equities, hedge funds and private equity. Notably, Leo structured cross-border financing transactions in Asia, originated and launched the first China A-share ETF listed on the Singapore Stock Exchange and developed innovative investment solutions such as the Dynamic Carry Index (DCI) while working at an international bank in 2004.

Leo's corporate experience includes a stint at a government institution, where he streamlined operations, refined policies, analysed investment projects and oversaw an investment portfolio with assets under management exceeding USD 500 million. Additionally, he has held CFO roles in various organisations. These roles involved raising Series A funding for a robotics company, enhancing processes, governance and financial management for a service-oriented company, and restructuring entities under judicial management for another.

In addition to his professional accomplishments in international finance, Leo is an avid artist. He shares his artwork on Instagram under the handle **Blink_Artstudio**.

Any feedback about this book can be sent to Instagram **leoderelephant**.

Made in the USA
Monee, IL
22 June 2025